Leo

23 July – 23 August

First published in Great Britain 2009
by Harlequin Mills & Boon Limited,
Eton House, 18-24 Paradise Road, Richmond, Surrey TW9 1SR

Copyright © Dadhichi Toth 2008 & 2009

ISBN: 978 0 263 87068 8

Typeset at Midland Typesetters Australia

Harlequin Mills & Boon policy is to use papers that are natural, renewable and recyclable products and made from wood grown in sustainable forests. The logging and manufacturing processes conform to the legal environmental regulations of the country of origin.

Printed and bound in Spain
by Litografia Rosés S.A., Barcelona

About
Dadhichi

Dadhichi is one of Australia's foremost astrologers. He has the ability to draw from complex astrological theory to provide clear, easily understandable advice and insights for people who want to know what their future might hold.

In the 26 years that Dadhichi has been practising astrology, face reading and other esoteric studies, he has conducted over 9,500 consultations. His clients include celebrities, political and diplomatic figures, and media and corporate identities from all over the world.

Dadhichi's unique blend of astrology and face reading helps people fulfil their true potential. His extensive experience practising western astrology is complemented by his research into the theory and practice of eastern systems of astrology.

Dadhichi features in numerous newspapers and magazines and he also appears regularly on many of Australia's leading television and radio networks, where many of his political and worldwide forecasts have proved uncannily accurate.

His website www.astrology.com.au is now one of the top ten online Australian lifestyle sites and, in conjunction with www.facereader.com, www.soulconnector.com and www.psychjuice.com, they attract over half a million visitors monthly. The websites offer a wide variety of features, helpful information and personal services.

Dedicated to The Light of Intuition
Sri V. Krishnaswamy—mentor and friend
With thanks to Julie, Joram, Isaac and Janelle

Welcome from
Dadhichi

Dear Friend,

Welcome! It's great to have you here, reading your horoscope, trying to learn more about yourself and what's in store for you in 2010.

I visited Mexico a while ago and stumbled upon the Mayan prophecies for 2012, which, they say, is the year when the longstanding calendar we use in the western world supposedly stops! If taken literally, some people could indeed believe that 'the end of the world is near'. However, I see it differently.

Yes, it might seem as though the world is getting harder and harder to deal with, especially when fear enters our lives. But, I believe that 'the end' indicated by these Mayan prophecies has more to do with the end that will create new beginnings for our societies, more to do with making changes to our material view of life and some necessary adjustments for the human race to progress and prosper in future. So let's get one thing straight: you and I will both be around after 2012, reading our 2013 horoscopes!

My prediction and advice centres around keeping a cool mind and not reacting to the fear that could overtake us. Of course, this isn't easy, especially when media messages might increase our anxiety about such things as the impacts of global warming or the scarcity of fossil fuels.

I want you to understand that it is certainly important to be aware and play your part in making the world a better place; however, the best and surest way to support global goals is to help yourself first. Let me explain. If everyone focused just a little more on improving *themselves* rather than just pointing their finger to criticise others, it would result in a dramatic change and improvement; not just globally, but societally. And, of course, you mustn't forget what a positive impact this would have on your personal relationships as well.

Astrology focuses on self-awareness; your own insights into your personality, thinking processes and relationships. This is why this small book you have in your hand doesn't only concentrate on what is going to happen, but more importantly how you can *make* things happen positively through being your best.

I have always said that there are two types of people: puppets and actors. The first simply react to each outside stimulus and are therefore slaves of their environment, and even of their own minds and emotions. They are puppets in the hands of karma. The other group I call actors. Although they can't control what happens to them all the time, either, they are better able to adapt and gain something purposeful in their lives. They are in no way victims of circumstance.

I hope you will use what is said in the following pages to become the master of your destiny, and not rely on the predictions that are given as mere fate but as valuable guidelines to use intelligently when life presents you with its certain challenges.

Neither the outside world, nor the ups and downs that occur in your life, should affect your innermost spirituality and self-confidence. Take control: look beyond your current challenges and use them as the building blocks of experience to create success and fulfilment in the coming year.

I believe you have the power to become great and shine your light for all to see. I hope your 2010 horoscope book will be a helpful guide and inspiration for you.

Warm regards, and may the stars shine brightly for you in 2010!

Your Astrologer,

Dadhichi Toth

Contents

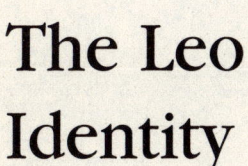

The Leo
Identity

There are two things to aim at in life: first to get what you want, and after that, to enjoy it. Only the wisest of mankind has achieved the second.

—Logan Pearsall Smith

Leo: A Snapshot

Key Characteristics

Pioneering, commanding, inflexible, ambitious, loyal, physical, generous, regal

Compatible Star Signs

Aries, Sagittarius, Gemini, Libra

Key Life Phrase

I shine

Life Goals

To set an example to others and lead with integrity

Platinum Assets

Great strength, vitality and magnetism

Zodiac Totem

The Lion

Zodiac Symbol

♌

Zodiac Facts

Fifth sign of the zodiac; fixed, hot, masculine, dry

Element

Fire

Famous Leos

Andy Warhol, Magic Johnson, Danielle Steel,
Billy Bob Thornton, Charlize Theron, Edward Norton,
Eric Bana, Geri Halliwell, J.K. Rowling, Halle Berry,
Hilary Swank, Kevin Spacey, Mick Jagger,
Sandra Bullock, Laurence Fishburne, Lisa Kudrow,
Arnold Schwarzenegger, Ben Affleck, Madonna,
Robert de Niro, Martha Stewart

Leo: Your profile

You will never be accused of lacking in self-confidence, that's for sure, Leo. Wherever you go, you make a strong impression and others never forget you. You have the ability to assert yourself and are a natural-born leader. Because of this, others tend to gravitate towards you and look up to you as a form of inspiration, giving them direction in their own lives. With this comes a great deal of responsibility, but you're not afraid to shoulder that burden because you like to be number one and in control of your own life … and sometimes others' lives as well.

You are ruled by the Sun, which is the central point of the solar system, around which all the other planets revolve. In like fashion, you are the centre of your universe and people gravitate towards you, using you as the fulcrum—the central support—of their own lives to a large extent. You are proud and, due to the adulation you will receive, can become quite vain, developing a rather large ego. Don't let the image of yourself cloud who you really are, even though others may find you very special.

Because of your innate strength, you have a tendency to gravitate towards others of equal strength. You mustn't let this override your compassion for those who are not quite as strong and confident as yourself.

You are creative; whether it is in business, socially, or within your own family itself, you are dramatic and like to express yourself in an individual manner. You hate being seen to be the same as others. You are unique, and you know it. And you want others to know it, too!

You are a dignified sort of individual with a great deal of self-respect, and honour also tops the list of those human traits you consider extremely important in life. If someone wounds your honour or humiliates you in any way, it is very difficult for you to forgive them and allow them back into your circle of trust.

You're a 'big picture' person and hate getting bogged down in trivia. One of your favourite sayings would be 'don't sweat the small stuff'. You prefer to keep your mind on bigger things and have an extraordinarily high level of ambition.

Early in life, you vowed to yourself that you'd be successful and may have even looked up to others who were rich, famous or successful in their own way. You've modelled yourself on these people and can't stand pettiness or negative thinking of any sort. You quickly disassociate from those who try to bring you down or have nothing better to do but whinge about how difficult life is.

While you're happy to give people a hand and to lead them and show them a better direction, you don't waste time on those who are not prepared to help themselves. In this way, you can seem rather heartless or cruel; but rather, this is because you believe your time and energy are valuable so you'd rather give them to those who are worthy.

You have one of the biggest hearts anyone could hope to find and your generosity is second to none. You give of yourself, your time and your resources, and are extremely loyal to the ones you love. You offer the strength and encouragement often lacking in close relationships and friendships, and people value you because of this.

You have an amazing love of life, immense physical vitality and such a positive outlook that your state of mind and the energy you exude is contagious to all around you. Like the Sun, you give light, life and warmth and are also usually quite impartial. Equally comfortable with someone in a high or low position, people appreciate your equality of vision.

Being born under Leo, you are an extremely

strong-willed person, determined to achieve what you set your mind to. Don't let your inflexibility and self-opinionated attitude alienate you from those who have different views. If you can extend yourself with a little more humility, the power of your Sun sign will work extraordinarily well to bring you additional happiness, success and friendship in life.

Generally speaking, the destiny for Leo is a good one, with success assured. The power of your own will and positive vibrations will attract everything you need in life.

Three classes of Leo

If you were born between the 24th of July and the 5th of August, the Sun rules you in greater measure than your Leo brothers and sisters. You are charismatic to say the least and will attract the right sort of people and circumstances into your life to give you a fulfilling and successful destiny. You may even find yourself occupying a high office, political portfolio, or at least will make it to the top of the pile in your chosen career.

If you're a Leo born between the 6th and 14th of August, you have a strong need for adventure and will look for ways to enhance your life. Travel and other activities that take you away from the humdrum of your day-to-day life will be necessary to fulfil you. Freedom and independence are the key words in the lives of Leos born during this period.

You must be careful not to let your impatience and anger get the better of you if you're a Leo born between the 15th and 23rd of August. You have the strong influence of Mars dominating your birth date and, therefore, you have the tendency to be reactive and also belligerent at times. You have a very warm and generous heart but need to be the boss. Your main lesson in life is humility.

Leo role model: Andy Warhol

Andy Warhol, the famous, progressive and some-times outlandish artist was a die-hard Leo, just like you. Desiring to be the centre of attention and dramatic in every respect, even in his personal life, Andy always wanted to be the best at what he did and to make an impact on the world. He sure did. He certainly reflects your true Leo spirit.

Leo: The light side

You have an extremely bright and attractive person-ality and people are naturally warmed by your presence. You are the one they look to when they're feeling flat and want an additional dose of good vibrations. Your dazzling presence uplifts everyone around you.

You are a dynamic individual who, even uncon-sciously, uplifts others through your words and actions. You're a generous person who likes to help others, but your generosity can sometimes exceed your ability to fulfil the increasing demands of people around you. Try to give a little bit of sunshine to yourself as well.

A born leader, you know exactly how to get from A to B and people are amazed at your determination. Like the king of the jungle, the lion, which is your totem, you take control of the circumstances around you and people are in awe of your ability to get things done.

You're extremely loyal and make a great family person. You nurture and support the ones you love but are also just as demanding in your need for attention and love in return. Leos have the power of persuasion so your words are able to sway the masses. Therefore, you should never underestimate the power that your words have over others. This power, coupled with your enthusiasm, will assure you of success and the brightest of destinies.

Leo: The shadow side

You are very opinionated and this makes you a little overbearing when it comes to putting forward your view. Your persistence and at times self-righteousness may be a little hard for others to handle. If people don't accept what you have to say, you'll still try to force your opinions down their throat, believing you are right.

Stubbornness is another attitude that needs to be kept in check because it can make you unable to accept that others have something of value to say based upon their experiences.

In your effort to be number one, you push yourself to the limits. This can sometimes take you away from the things you cherish most, like your family. For example, you work long and hard to achieve the benefits of your professional activities, not just for yourself but for the ones you care for most. However, there's no point going through all this if you can't enjoy the benefits of your hard work or the love your family has to offer you. Try to make more time for them.

In your attempt to be the centre of attention, you can disregard the needs of others. Open your heart to develop a wider sensitivity to what might be happening to people around you.

Leo woman

Women born under the sign of Leo are extraordinarily unique. The powerful radiations of the Sun imbue you with incredible personal pride, lightness of being and immense physical energy as well.

You can't turn away from a Leo woman when you see her in the crowd. Her persona and physical presence is a mixture of nobility, a bright aura and straightforward honesty. If you were born under Leo and you are a woman, you have a charismatic appeal to which others are naturally drawn.

You dress impeccably, have a stylish way about you, and can command respect without even saying a word. There is something regal about your physical presence and others notice this about you immediately.

When it comes to friends and love, one of the primary requirements for you is that you have admiration or respect for others. Unless you feel some sort of honour for another person, you don't feel right associating with them. This has to do with the very high standard you set for yourself. You are sincere in your manner, ambitious and intelligent, and expect those of your peer group to have the same standards and aspirations that you do.

Being born under the fire sign of Leo means you have an extra dose of passion, not just sexually but in every aspect of your life. You are attentive and diligent as well as creative in your endeavours. This passion is seen in the way you approach your work as well as your personal relationships. You never do things half-heartedly and this sometimes makes others appear to be less than capable in their approach to things.

You must be careful not to let these powerful attributes of your character get others offside. Many Leo women end up making enemies—not through any fault of their own but rather for quite the opposite reason—for being just too adept and setting a standard that is way too high for others to achieve.

You do expect the best from yourself and others, but you are probably a little naïve in thinking that others generally aspire to the same level of excellence that you do. Try to make your expectations a little more realistic. By all means, demand the best of yourself, but don't insist on it too much from others because you'll probably be severely disappointed.

You are sometimes unaware of the fact that your impeccable sense of self-presentation, drama and creativity is regarded as vanity by others. You could be hurt to learn that some of those whom you trust and admire might regard you in this way. Therefore you must develop a heightened awareness and sensitivity to what others are saying between their lines. Also, try not to exaggerate any facts because others also see this as a trait in you that needs to be curtailed.

You love to be pampered and are not averse to flattery but you must never, under any circumstances, make these the criteria for your own inner fulfilment. By all means accept compliments, but learn to rely on your own self-confidence and self-assurance for your personal happiness. Finally, try not to be too authoritative or arrogant. Control yourself and develop humility, as this is one of the main spiritual lessons for you in life.

Leo man

People are taken aback by your strong opinions and just how self-assured you are when you speak.

They probably wonder if you truly believe everything you say because of the forcefulness with which you present it. At times, this could come across as a basic insecurity and a need to overcompensate.

Actually, you do believe in what you say but you're so enthusiastic and excited about what it is you need to convey that at times you embellish it or possibly even exaggerate the facts without knowing it. You must pay more attention to expressing the truth as it is without any of the additional frills. You will thereby gain even greater respect from others.

As a man born under the sign of Leo, there's never a dull moment in your life. You hate to remain still and believe that life is to be lived. The fruits of life and, through your labour, the achievements you gain, are the purpose of living. You therefore never hold back from giving 100 per cent to what you choose to do or to any person you desire to give your heart and mind. Energy, vitality, courage and earnestness are your key words and this causes you to do your best and to help others do their best as well.

Competition is an important aspect of your personality, which is why many great sportsmen are born under the sign of Leo. You love to play, to compete and most of all to win, but generally you have a pretty good sense of fair play and sportsmanship. You enjoy a game, whether it is on a football field or playing a hand of cards. Socialising and blending this competitive instinct of yours will promise a rich and fulfilling social life and lifestyle generally.

You are the king of the jungle, the lion, and therefore need to be in a position where you can exert your influence and authority. You want to be in the limelight and you're not scared to take on the biggest of roles to prove to yourself and everyone else that you can do it!

You are a born actor and can easily convince even the most sceptical person that what you have in mind, your ideas and your direction, are the correct ones for all concerned. Sometimes you even dupe yourself into believing you can do something only to find out later that the task is much bigger and the journey will take a little longer. However, this doesn't bother you and in fact spurs you on to give even more of yourself to achieve your desired goals.

You're able to project your personality onto your surroundings easily and this is what marks you apart from others. You like to show others how it can be done. Even under the most trying of circumstances, you rise to the occasion and inspire others with the unending vitality of yours. You truly are an inspiration.

Your sex appeal is strong because you are a passionate individual with a very strong will as well. Women are attracted to this and most Leo men like to play the field and enjoy the variety of sexual pleasures that life can offer. You are not averse to exploring the wilder side of your nature, either.

Strength, vitality, generosity and a shining personality are the prominent character traits that make you, Leo, destined for great things in life.

Leo child

You couldn't find a happier child than the child of Leo. Having their birth in the period of the Sun, the average Leo child is naturally playful, competitive and exuberant, loving of life and drawn to others with whom they can share these qualities.

You might have some difficulties at the outset with your Leo child and this stems from their need for continual attention. However, you mustn't disregard them because this will wound their joyful little spirits. By the same token, you mustn't give in and pander to their excessive need for adulation. Treat them fairly with kindness and give them the approval that is necessary without spoiling them.

Criticising a child of Leo is also something that needs to be done with considerable tact and diplomacy. The Leo that is hurt unnecessarily will turn in on him- or herself, making it hard for you to draw them back out again. This will also cause them to rebel against authority, making life difficult for them in school and in their social lives.

Leo children are the centre of their social circle and friends love to be with them. They are dignified and have an air of nobility about them. They are charismatic and generally outgoing in their personalities and so this is a natural fit for a healthy social life.

Teaching your Leo child the art of sharing is essential because they tend to dominate their peer group, not giving others the chance to express themselves. They won't want to choose the game, the time, the location of play and so forth, only to find out their friends become intimidated by them and aren't able to express their desires and needs. Teaching your Leo child the benefits of give and take will help them, especially if you can do that in the early stages of their development.

A balance of loving hugs and authority that doesn't diminish their ability to stand on their own two feet is essential in the nurturing and personality development of your Leo child. As they grow older, they will challenge their teachers by knowing more than anyone else. As long as you can advise them in the ways of humility, sharing and truth telling, your Leo child will grow up to be a well-integrated being.

Romance, love and marriage

Leo is one of the most romantic lovers of the zodiac. If you are born under this sign, you know exactly what I'm talking about when I say you need to express your love and to receive it in equal amounts. Unless there is a warm and mutual experience emotionally, mentally and physically, you will never be satisfied in your love life. Love and romance is one of the most natural activities for you.

Because the Sun and Leo rules the fifth zone of the zodiac, which relates to entertainment, playful sports and creativity, your love affairs will naturally involve all of these aspects of life. Seriousness and conservatism in your romantic attitudes will, for the most part, be conspicuously absent. You need joy, humour, lightness and playfulness as the foundation of what you consider to be a happy and fulfilling relationship.

Socially, you are the centre of attention, whether you're a man or a woman. Leo has no problem attracting lovers, even into old age. You always exude the prowess of the lion or lioness of the jungle and will dominate your social circumstances to an extent that others feel they don't have much of a chance in competing with you for the best partners on offer. Sometimes people will misinterpret your motivation and could see you as muscling in on their territory, simply for the sake of proving that you can. Don't be arrogant in love and try to be graceful when it comes to competing for the hand of someone else in romance or marriage.

Because you are an extrovert and dramatic in your manner, you exert such a powerful force on others that they sometimes feel intimidated to the extent that they feel you're above them. You may meet someone who is perfect for you, only to find that they shy away, thinking you will reject them.

Try to tone down your manner, at least in the initial stages of your romance, so that you give the other person a chance to see into who you really are. You don't want to scare away your soulmate before you actually have a chance of getting to know them a little better, do you?

Leo is extremely loyal in love and once you have found someone you consider your life partner, you will give 100 per cent of your heart and soul to them. Being warm and affectionate, you'll desire to serve them in any way you can. However, by the same token, you expect the same in return. You won't be satisfied with someone who's half-hearted and lacking in demonstrativeness. You'll quickly look for another partner if your physical as well as emotional needs are not fulfilled.

Sexuality is of primary importance to you, and your partner must understand that you'll need loads of physical attention to feel good about yourself. If you select someone who is insipid and lacking in physical drive, you may have difficulty in sustaining a relationship.

Because you make such a great impression in any given situation and you have such a wonderful fashion sense, you'll be extraordinarily lucky in love. Even if you don't make a conscious effort to attract people, you just seem to have the knack of drawing people towards you. Some Leos marry young and this is because your naturally protective and even territorial instincts are such ingrained parts of your personality.

In love, you must never become possessive because this will create difficulties in your marital life. Try to listen as much as you talk and give the other person a chance to exert their influence in the social circle. In love, you may try to dominate the situation and this, over time, will only end up undermining the satisfaction you should be able to enjoy with all the wonderful, emotional and sensual attributes that you as a Leo possess.

Health, wellbeing and diet

You probably take your health and vitality for granted, being as strong and vital as you are. Leo rarely has trouble on the physical level and if there is a problem from time to time, it's more than likely a result of your overdoing it rather than having anything intrinsically wrong with your body.

Another reason you can look forward to a healthy and long life is because of your love of sport and other outdoor pastimes. You are naturally attracted to physical movement, fresh air, bushwalks and other activities that keep your body mobile, your blood moving and your overall health in a good state.

Moderation will be important for you as you do tend to overdo things, working hard and playing even harder. By applying this principle of the middle path of moderation, you'll enhance your health and wellbeing even more.

The areas of the spine, the back and the heart are the principal areas ruled by the sign of Leo. Because of your tendency to overexert, you may injure these parts of your body so try to pay attention to your posture and never overstrain yourself at the gym or when it comes to lifting heavy objects.

Your cardiovascular system is also an area you need to pay attention to. This can be done through a balanced diet.

Spicy dishes containing chilli and/or curry can 'overheat' your metabolism. Try to take adequate liquids to keep your system a little cooler, especially if you like these sorts of hot and fiery foods. Leo the lion is a carnivore, therefore you generally enjoy eating meat. If you choose a vegetarian diet, you'll need to be careful to eat enough high quality vegetable protein foods.

Whole grains and fresh vegetables are obviously perfect for your diet, and you should try to avoid processed foods so as to neutralise any excess acidity in your system. Supplementary herbs and vitamins help augment your health and these include lime juice, chamomile and fenugreek. These will help to detoxify your body, especially if you do eat meat.

Papaya, mango, banana and all the other yellow- or gold-coloured fruits are in sync with your Leo temperament. Orange vegetables such as pumpkin are also excellent for your health. Try to focus on wholegrain rice if you need to eat starchy grains. This will further increase your wellbeing.

Work

Because you're born under the fixed sign of Leo, you have an incredible drive and determination to organise your life in a way that fulfils you and makes you feel successful. You are decisive in your approach to work and have profound powers of concentration.

The contribution of the fire sign of Aries makes you ambitious, enthusiastic and driven. Add to this your creative element and you make an ideal employee or someone who generally will want to work independently to achieve their ambitions.

When people work with you, they realise straightaway that you're a person of integrity who acts honestly, works fairly and demands the same high principles of integrity in equal return from co-workers, employers and clients alike.

Working in a subservient position causes you great dissatisfaction, which is why you will very quickly move up the ranks of your career to occupy a powerful and even influential position. You like a good lifestyle and to do this you need to earn a lot of money. You will be able to fulfil these basic aspirations.

Because you are so dramatic, a career in theatre and the entertainment industry would be ideal for you. Also, work in sales and marketing or any type of executive position in which you control the situation will bring you professional satisfaction.

Key to karma, spirituality and emotional balance

Your past life experiences affect this present life and, because Aries is strongly associated to your previous life, it has made you who you are. Your need for power and control is part of your character. Balancing these personality traits will be your karmic challenge.

Your key words are 'I shine', and shine you do, but another challenge is to balance your desire for approval with humility and self-satisfaction. Learning to share the glory with others will help you grow spiritually.

On Sundays and Thursdays, connect with your inner powers of intuition and psychic abilities. Ruby and garnet are helpful gemstones for Leo.

Your lucky days

Your luckiest days are Sundays, Mondays, Tuesdays and Thursdays.

Your lucky numbers

Remember that the forecasts given later in the book will help you optimise your chances of winning. Your lucky numbers are:

1, 10, 19, 28, 37, 46, 55

3, 12, 21, 30, 39, 48, 57

9, 18, 27, 36, 45, 54, 63

Your destiny years

Your most important years are 1, 10, 19, 28, 37, 46, 55, 64, 73 and 82.

Star Sign
Compatibility

*In the absence of clearly defined goals, we become
strangely loyal to performing daily acts of trivia.*

—Author unknown

Romantic compatibility

How compatible are you with your current partner,
lover or friend? Did you know that astrology can
reveal a whole new level of understanding between
people simply by looking at their star sign and that
of their partner? In this chapter I'd like to share
some special insights that will help you better
appreciate your strengths and challenges using Sun
sign compatibility.

The Sun reflects your drive, willpower and
personality. The essential qualities of two star signs
blend like two pure colours, producing an entirely
new colour. Relationships, similarly, produce their
own emotional colours when two people interact.
The following is a general guide to your romantic
prospects with others and how, by knowing the
astrological 'colour' of each other, the art of love
can help you create a masterpiece.

When reading the following I ask you to remember
that no two star signs are ever *totally* incompatible.
With effort and compromise, even the most 'difficult' astrological matches can work. Don't close
your mind to the full range of life's possibilities!
Learning about each other and ourselves is the
most important facet of astrology.

Quick-reference guide: Horoscope compatibility between signs (percentage)

	Aries	Taurus	Gemini	Cancer	Leo	Virgo	Libra	Scorpio	Sagittarius	Capricorn	Aquarius	Pisces
Aries	60	65	70	65	90	45	70	80	90	50	55	65
Taurus	65	70	70	80	70	90	75	85	50	95	80	85
Gemini	70	70	75	60	80	75	90	60	75	50	90	50
Cancer	65	80	60	75	70	75	60	95	55	45	70	90
Leo	90	70	80	70	85	75	65	75	95	45	70	75
Virgo	45	90	75	75	75	70	80	85	70	95	50	70
Libra	70	75	90	60	65	80	80	85	80	85	95	50
Scorpio	80	85	60	95	75	85	85	90	85	65	60	95
Sagittarius	90	50	75	55	95	70	80	80	85	55	60	75
Capricorn	50	95	50	45	45	95	85	65	55	85	70	85
Aquarius	55	80	90	70	70	50	60	95	60	70	80	55
Pisces	65	85	50	90	75	70	50	95	75	85	55	80

Each star sign combination is followed by the elements of those star signs and the result of their combining. For instance, Aries is a fire sign and Aquarius is an air sign and this combination produces a lot of 'hot air'. Air feeds fire and fire warms air. In fact, fire requires air. However, not all air and fire combinations work. I have included information about the different birth periods within each star sign and this will throw even more light on your prospects for a fulfilling love life with any star sign you choose.

Good luck in your search for love, and may the stars shine upon you in 2010!

Compatibility quick-reference guide

Each of the twelve star signs has a greater or lesser affinity with one another. The quick-reference guide will show you who's hot and who's not so hot as far as your relationships are concerned.

LEO + ARIES

Fire + Fire = Explosion

A romantic alliance between Leo and Aries is one of the best in the zodiac. The two of you have complete respect and admiration for each other because you are both intensely powerful star signs. When fire signs join forces, it results in an incredibly vital and productive combination.

You're both quite ambitious and you will find

Aries is supportive, if not helpful, to you in achieving your goals. You'll be in sync with each other and, although you may have the odd clash or two because you're both quite opinionated, the relationship should, for the most part, go quite smoothly.

Aries has a 'me first' attitude, which might present some problems in terms of rulership in the household and the partnership generally. One of you may have to concede that the other is more dominant in the partnership and this could be difficult because your egos are both so strong.

In the course of the relationship, this will give rise to competitive stand-offs and so part of your lesson together will be that of humility and conceding that you are not always right nor in a position to dominate the other. Unfortunately, Aries is not always a gracious loser, so you'll have to teach them the art of fair play in love.

One of the other drawbacks with your relationship is that your high level of energy might create differences in the way you want to live your lives. Too much fire can burn you out. The positive side of this is that sexually you are both expressive and want to please each other.

On a sexual level you will be extremely in tune with each other and want to demonstrate exactly how you feel. You'll believe your needs are met by your fire partner and that you are appreciated for what you have to offer them.

The fire signs are quite spontaneous and creative. On every level of your beings, you will feel that this is the case and so the relationship should never get stale. You will both lead an excessive lifestyle overindulging your senses, so you need to take care that this aspect of your lives doesn't interfere in the stability of creating a happy family life.

There's a great attraction with Arians born between the 21st and 30th of March. These individuals have a very strong Martian influence and it shows that you are both destined to meet and develop the relationship. You're curious about these individuals and will have something important to learn from them. This is definitely a relationship that can fulfil both of you.

Generally speaking, Aries is a great sign for you in every respect but you'll find that those born between the 31st of March and the 10th of April are even better suited to your temperament. You'll be very easily enticed by their winning ways. You'll see many aspects of your personality mirrored in theirs. There's an intuitive connection between you and both of you will often know what the other is thinking or feeling.

With Aries born between the 11th and the 20th of April, you also find a great deal of satisfaction. These individuals love to be out and about, always travelling and socialising. You will want to be part of the action with them. The sexual relationship between you is also excellent.

LEO + TAURUS

Fire + Earth = Lava

The signs of Leo and Taurus superficially seem to be compatible with each other; however, if you scratch beneath the surface, there are some very distinct differences in your personalities. Relationships require more than the social pizzazz that you may experience together.

Taurus is very steady, plodding, and at times unable to change in their ways. You, Leo, on the other hand, want someone who can stimulate you, who's prepared to try different things and this may not always work with a Taurean partner.

You're attracted to each other, there's no doubt about that. However, once the relationship settles down into its habitual routine, you'll start to see these differences emerging. One important factor here is the fixity of both your signs. You are both in your own ways very stubborn and are not prepared to change to accommodate the other person's views or philosophies. This will cause you to clash and a battle of wills may ensue on many fronts. The lifelong lesson you will need to learn with each other is that of flexibility and respect.

If you're prepared to put aside these differences and to really work hard at the relationship, there are some particularly excellent traits that you have going for you. Both the signs of Leo and Taurus are loyal and supportive. You have a great deal of self-confidence and this can be utilised well by Taurus, who is sometimes a little shy and unable to assert themselves. Taurus, on the other hand, is very practical and security conscious and can make you feel grounded and looked after. In terms of a family life together, you can create a situation that is protective and fully nurturing for yourselves and your children.

Both of you are sensual and this aspect of the relationship with Taurus will most certainly please you. Taurus is one of the most sensual signs of the zodiac, being ruled by Venus. Your passions will drive Taurus wild. Their soft, loving and sensual ways will inspire you.

There are many pros and cons in the Leo and Taurus relationship. You're quite open and dramatic in your manner and the patient and plodding Taurus might possibly be a little overpowered by your Leo traits.

A relationship with Taureans born between the 21st and the 29th of April will attract you due to their very sensual and sexual nature. They are, however, slower off the mark than you, and also opinionated and unable to adapt their views to your satisfaction. This will frustrate you. It will be *you* that will have to change, not them. Are you able to do that?

Those under the sign of Taurus born between the 30th of April and the 10th of May will fare much better with you, romantically speaking. They will take an interest in your social life and also help you professionally.

A relationship with Taureans born between the 11th and the 21st of May is a good one. You love family life and mutually work hard to satisfy each other. This is one Leo–Taurus combination that can actually work.

LEO + GEMINI

Fire + Air = Hot Air

Love with Gemini can be a lot of fun. You have a natural attraction to the lovely and mentally stimulating star sign of Gemini.

Friendship exists between the two of you because the sign of Gemini falls in the eleventh zone of friendships in the zodiac to Leo. Most astrologers would agree this is a very good combination and one that provides a good foundation for not just friendship but love and possibly even marriage.

However, a love affair with Gemini needs time to settle down because they can be rather scattered, wanting to do many things at once. Socially and communicatively, they are like monkeys, jumping from tree to tree. Keeping up with them will be a real challenge for you. This being said, you do enjoy their interesting banter and the way they connect well with people on a social level. Sticking to one thing is really the main problem here, even in terms of their friendships. They love to skim the surface and explore different options. This might make you feel a little unsteady at times.

Money can be a problem for Leo and Gemini, with Gemini gaining at your expense. This is a karmic issue and indicates that, as the relationship becomes deeper and deeper, you may find your professional or financial affairs becoming unsettled. Get together regularly to talk about your financial differences so that things don't spiral out of control.

Gemini enjoys your mental agility and dramatic flair and you like to take centre stage. Gemini is quite happy to allow you this enjoyment. Gemini supports your creativity and this works wonderfully well. Your skills and personalities complement each other perfectly and your mutual appreciation and respect works to both of your advantages.

Geminis born between the 22nd of May and the 1st of June will be a great asset to your business and money-making aspirations. As well as being great friends, you'll work creatively together to produce some incredible ideas. Mostly, you can direct these concepts to making money together and this will provide you with long-term security as a couple.

A class of Geminis born between the 2nd and the 12th of June are very attractive to you and vice versa. You have common social interests and you'll both want to take full advantage of this to further your careers. Leo, you have a very strong constitution, but with these individuals, you may be tested when trying to keep up with them.

With Geminis born between the 13th and 21st of June you have an excellent choice of partner for marriage. Aquarius, the radical and progressive sign of the zodiac, co-rules these individuals and therefore their crazy antics will attract you and keep you stimulated, young at heart and ever-creative together. Your meeting might be in one of the most unusual or unexpected scenarios.

LEO + CANCER

Fire + Water = Steam

Here again we see a very different quality between you and another star sign; that is, Cancer. Cancer is a water sign and you are a fire sign. Likewise, your temperaments are radically different and therefore a great deal of adjustment is necessary if you are to make a go of a relationship together.

You always expect people to accept your honesty as some sort of consolation prize for being with you. But think again with a Cancer, one of the most sensitive signs of the zodiac, ruled by the Moon and the element of water. Your energy may be a little too powerful for them and your direct, sometimes brutal honesty may leave them wounded if you're not careful.

If you have to present the truth to Cancer, do so bearing in mind their moody nature and their inability to take it in all at once. A softer approach is absolutely necessary when dealing with the Cancerian personality.

Cancer is the type of person who will serve you well in life and be quite happy for you to steal the limelight and receive all the adulation. That's okay, as long as you are prepared to give them some recognition, even though it may be in private, for their contributions to your success.

Your relationship with Cancer can be sensual and that will be evident from the outset. They are soft, loving and nurturing individuals and you will love the fact that they know just how to make you feel good. As long as you are able to listen selectively to what they have to say and can also handle their somewhat dramatic mood changes, you'll probably go far with Cancer.

Given time, your sexual relationship can work well but you may be a little impatient in waiting for them to warm to you. Don't forget: water, Cancer's element, may put out the passionate flames of your Leo sexuality. You need to remember that love is not always expressed in the way *you* want to express it. There are other ways of sharing your deepest feelings and you need to accommodate this in your Cancer partner.

You have some wonderful romantic interludes with Cancerians born between the 14th and the 23rd of July. These individuals love to give of themselves and you feel comfortable because of your own generosity. These characters are selfless in that they wish to please, so you mustn't take advantage of this but learn to reciprocate and give as much as you take.

There is a group of Cancerians who are particularly inflexible and also very emotionally demanding. They are born between the 4th and the 13th of July. They have a touch of Scorpio in their personalities so they can also be possessive and at times vindictive.

Relationships with Cancers born between the 22nd of June and the 3rd of July are not particularly easy. They are very idealistic and expect so much more of a relationship. You feel as though there's nothing you'll do that will ever satisfy them. This will frustrate you no end.

LEO + LEO

Fire + Fire = Explosion

When two individuals are born under the same star sign, it means that the elements of their Sun signs are the same. This is a wonderful start to a relationship, ensuring a higher success rate for them in the romance stakes. This is the case with Leo and Leo.

Both of you have an incredibly attractive charm, willpower, and big egos to match! Although you are immediately attracted to each other, it won't be long before you realise you've met your equal and will have a lot of work to do to humble yourself enough to accommodate someone whose ego, head and heart are as big as yours.

A relationship between two egos is usually built on mutual admiration and ego-building. This is fine, but once you break through all of this initial backslapping you'll realise that considerable effort is needed to develop a long-term relationship together.

Both of you are demanding in terms of the attention that you need. You are sometimes self-centred; self-absorbed in your work and your ambitions, to the exclusion of others. You are the centre of the solar system and in the same way may find yourself constantly feeling that the universe should revolve around you. But there's a problem: there is only one universe. Therefore, with two Leos together, whose universe are we talking about, and which of you is it going to revolve around?

Although there are power conflicts here, we might say that the two of you in company are like a binary star—blazing brightly for all to see. This is a combination that is unmistakable and spectacular. The two of you will be the centre of attention in your social circle, making a great impression wherever you go.

Because you're both spiritual, you have an innate understanding and want to develop your own personal selves in unison. Your emotional, intellectual as well as spiritual growth can be accelerated by your relationship together.

Humility is the karmic lesson for both of you. Once you learn to humble yourself and give the other a chance to express their inner needs, this relationship will start to take off and fulfil you at the deepest level. Don't be superficial; look to the needs of your partner and the karmic returns will be immense.

With Leos born between the 24th of July and the 5th of August, you'll experience head-on confrontations due to their obstinate and egotistical natures. This breed of Leo is particularly stubborn and so you'll have to work harder to adjust to their needs if you are to be happy with them.

Natives of Leo born between the 6th and 14th of August are not as aggressive or dominant as other Leos and therefore, tuning into them and developing a relationship with them will be satisfactory, bringing friendship and loads of laughs as well. This will be an enjoyable partnership.

With Leos born between the 15th and the 23rd of August, you will also experience some intense clashes of will. These are a complex, hard to understand bunch of Leos, but nevertheless you'll still be attracted to them. The outcome for a relationship with them is not too fortunate and could in fact be unstable and disappointing in the end.

LEO + VIRGO

Fire + Earth = Lava

It's quite surprising, to say the least, that you'd be attracted to Virgo. I say this because they are usually quite shy and simple people who don't have the same sort of creative, dramatic or social flair that Leos do. Perhaps it's something in them that you admire; something you'd like to develop in yourself that initially draws you to them.

Virgo needs to know the reasons for everything. They are analytical by nature, both in terms of their work and the people they associate themselves with. You shouldn't be taken aback or insulted when they start scrutinising you and questioning you to the nth degree. You could be a little uncomfortable, thinking that Virgo is putting you down. You mustn't take it like this. Be open about your shortcomings and Virgo will appreciate you more.

Virgo is concerned with the details, whereas you're a 'big picture' person. At times you'll get a little annoyed having to deal with such minutiae, but that is something you need to get used to if you're going to be involved with a Virgo for a lengthy period of time.

Virgo is happy to sit in the background and watch you enjoy others inflating your ego. In fact, they'll probably serve you better than anyone else in this respect. They will ground you because they are an earth sign. And that's why the Leo–Virgo combination can work quite well. You'll be surprised that they don't expect too much from you and are happy to give, give and give a little bit more. Don't abuse their generosity, however.

Virgo is slow to warm up sexually. But, once you win their hearts, you will appreciate the fact that they are a great deal more passionate and demonstrative than anyone could have ever thought. This will in turn stimulate you to respond to them even more, and so on and so forth. Virgo is probably not your best partner between the sheets, but if you are the type of person who is looking for more than just sexual and physical gratification, Virgo might just be the all-round type of sign that satisfies you in eight out of ten areas.

Your attraction to Virgos born between the 24th of August and the 2nd of September will work well. They are not quite as highly strung as typical Virgos and you enjoy their quick minds and lively discussions.

With Virgos born between the 3rd and 12th of September, you find communication and even just hanging out with them a little difficult. This is due to the influence of Saturn on them. It might just be too much hard work trying to loosen them up and bringing them out of their shell.

You're quite attracted to Virgos born between the 13th and the 23rd of September. They have a stronger personality than some of their other Virgo brothers and sisters and you'll have to expect some clashes and arguments with them. They are more assertive than you think at first and their domineering ways may be a little too much for you to handle.

LEO + LIBRA

Fire + Air = Hot Air

Libra needs love. It thrives on the attention that someone like you can give them. Leo is warm, bright and uplifting. You're able to sweep up everyone around you with your confidence and your enthusiasm. The two of you together will make a beautiful couple and these Leo traits, coupled with the Libran style, harmony and goodwill, make you a couple that is sought after in any social situation. You'll have plenty of friends together.

Diplomacy is one of the key character traits of Libra. This is why the scales of justice are used as the symbol of Libra, indicating balance (or does that mean a striving to balance?). The fact of the matter is that some Librans are a little unstable and this is again due to the fact that they were born under the element of air. They can be chatterboxes sometimes, which may drive you wild. You enjoy good conversation but Libra may tire you with their endless discussions and intellectual curiosity.

Because Libra is concerned with justice, your honesty and fairness is respected by them. If you're hanging out with Libra, though, remember that their priorities in life are peace and harmony, so any sort of confrontation or begging for an argument will fall on deaf ears. They're more likely to walk away than come right out in a fight.

No doubt there is a powerful attraction between you, and the charisma you both exude means that you connect very easily. This is an excellent combination for a long-term partnership or marriage and brings with it both emotional and material welfare.

The two of you have a common interest in socialising, going to functions, and preparing dinners for friends at home and, therefore, your domestic life will incorporate many of these social activities. You are both houseproud and enjoy making your family and home life the hub of entertainment for friends.

The karma between you and Librans born between the 4th and the 13th of October is very powerful. You like their slightly zany attitude because they are spontaneous, independent and always come up with something creatively quirky. These people will always keep you on your toes.

Librans born between the 24th of September and the 3rd of October also have a great compatibility rating with you. They're always running here, there and everywhere and cannot be tied down.

Don't try to pigeonhole them or this will bring down your relationship. As long as you can give them the freedom they want, the relationship will go smoothly.

You have a moderately good relationship with Librans born between the 14th and the 23rd of October. They are co-ruled by Mercury, a changeable, dual planet, which means that their moods might swing like a pendulum. You 'won't know whether you're 'Arthur or Martha' as a result.

LEO + SCORPIO

Fire + Water = Steam

You admire power in another person, which is why Scorpio will attract you. Their deep and strong manner complements your own level of willpower and self-confidence.

Ordinarily, astrologers wouldn't say that Leo and Scorpio are particularly a good match, but in my own experience, I've found this one defies the traditional view. Leo and Scorpio can indeed work well together in many cases.

Scorpio nurtures your body, mind and spirit. Although you are both fixed signs in the zodiac, which means considerable stubbornness from both of you, you do feel comfortable together and are able to draw from each other's strengths. Scorpio is complex, emotionally. They will absorb your bright, sunny rays of solar energy and, in this way, you can balance each other inwardly and outwardly.

You appreciate the psychological depths of the Scorpio mind. They are deep, complex and intuitive and this stimulates your pursuit of meaning in life. You understand each other on an emotional level but Scorpio also has the added advantage of being one of the most psychic signs. This intrigues you and you want to know more about how to develop this untapped part of your nature.

Overall, the Leo–Scorpio combination produces a very happy family environment. The reason for this is that Scorpio is the fourth sign to Leo, indicating domestic happiness, real estate and family life in general. For this reason, the relationship (if it can overcome some of the more stubborn and inflexible aspects of your personalities) can provide for a very happy, long-term marital affair.

With Scorpios born between the 3rd and the 12th of November, you have a great sense of camaraderie. This is a very good combination for you, Leo; your spirit and your mind will feel nourished by the powerful Scorpio emotion.

Scorpios are keen to assert their control in a relationship. You too like to assert yourself but if you team up with someone born between the 13th and the 22nd of November, you may have to concede that they are a little stronger. Apart from this, they are also quite sensitive and philosophical in temperament.

There is a breed of Scorpios born between the 24th of October and the 2nd of November who are extremely sexually alluring and emotionally intense. They have very powerful, sensual appetites and, if you get involved with them, you need to be prepared to spend many long, loving hours in their company, satisfying these primal needs.

LEO + SAGITTARIUS

Fire + Fire = Explosion

There aren't too many power combinations in the zodiac that work well, but a relationship between Leo and Sagittarius is destined to be one of great success and fulfilment for both of you. Being fire signs, you reciprocate each other's warmth, power, love and enjoyment of a laugh.

Sagittarius is the fifth sign to Leo, indicating play, competition and sport. In other words, a relationship between you and a Sagittarian can be one of great fun and enjoyment.

Karma between Leo and Sagittarius is also very strong and, in the moment you meet, in that instant where you first set eyes upon each other, you will feel a deep and loving connection. There will be no doubt in either of your minds that you've known each other before and that it's time to continue from where you left off.

Sagittarius loves your enthusiastic and radiant attitude and you equally enjoy their free, loving and independent spirits. Both of you have a lust for life and will spend a lot of time exploring the world together as friends and lovers.

The Sagittarian spirit of exploration and travel turns you on. You hate boredom and therefore you'll instantly realise that Sagittarius is one of those people who will stimulate your mind and your interest in things beyond your immediate environment. Together you can travel and enjoy numerous, varied adventures.

You may demand a little more in terms of commitment from Sagittarius, who is sometimes less than willing in this regard, especially in the early stages of a relationship. However, exercise more patience and there's no doubt that the element of fire, which is in both of you, will join up so they will feel completely at ease and comfortable in giving their hearts over to you for the long term.

If you choose to work together, you'll do it in a creative capacity, bouncing off each other's ideas and inspiring each other to do your best. This can result in a successful business enterprise if you choose to team up commercially. This creative spark is no less evident in your personal lives as well, where your spare time together will be one of endeavouring to improve on yourselves and your relationship day by day.

Sagittarians born between the 12th and the 22nd of December attract you because they too have a strong connection to the Sun and Leo. You truly identify with these individuals and will naturally be attracted to them, seeing much of your own personality and character reflected in them.

If you happen to connect yourself with a Sagittarian born between the 23rd November and the 1st of December, passion and sexual energy will be extremely powerful between you. You are both intense personalities and I see this as an almost perfect match for your fiery and intense love. This is a relationship that is sensually very satisfying.

With Sagittarians born between the 2nd and the 11th of December, you have a great deal in common and this goes beyond the physical. Your spiritual and philosophical connectivity will be the foundation of your love and life together. Both of you learn extremely important lessons in unison and will be transformed in the process.

LEO + CAPRICORN

Fire + Earth = Lava

Like a gambler on the stock market, when planning a relationship with a Capricorn, you may find yourself investing considerable energy with little in return. If you're a punter and like to gamble, then by all means, entertain the notion of love with Capricorn. The odds of feeling satisfied with a Capricorn are very slim for Leo.

You are outgoing and have a solar temperament; that is, you are ruled by the life-giving, warm and vital Sun. Capricorn, on the other hand, is dominated by the solitary and serious, but also traditional, Saturn. They are not as extroverted as you and this could end up being a full-time job, trying to bring them out of their shell. In fact, you will find it quite disconcerting at times, being in the company of someone who appears cool and aloof and not at all concerned with your spontaneous and dramatic antics.

On the one hand, you are not at all compatible; yet on the other, especially in the company of other people, Capricorn will give you as much rope as you need to hang yourself. They're quite happy to let you steal the show while they sit back and calmly, solemnly, observe the outcome of these social engagements.

Your contrasting energies are likely to work together but the compromises you have to make will be so great that you'll probably not find this a lasting or fulfilling affair.

Capricorn is an excellent moneymaker, being traditional about their material values and, if you like a stable and secure future with lots of luxury to go with your lifestyle, you might sacrifice everything else for the sake of material success. But ... I don't think so.

Sexually, you are also very different and may not feel all that comfortable with each other. Capricorn, who is conservative, seeking a slower and steadier pace, may not fulfil you with your strong and vibrant demands. Capricorn, on the other hand, will feel satisfied by your warmth and energy.

Capricorns born between the 23rd of December and the 1st of January will not be a good match for you. These Capricorns are the typical traditional, cool-as-cucumber types, who may leave you high and dry. Being extremely suspicious by nature, you'll find yourself walking on eggshells to please them. It's probably best not to invest too much time and energy into this relationship.

With Capricorns born between the 2nd and the 10th of January, however, you must make an exception about the sexual and intimate responses that you'll find with them. They are marginally more expressive than the general group of Capricorns.

You have fine communicative interaction with Capricorns born between the 11th and 20th of January. A high degree of friendship is also noted in this combination and, if you choose to work professionally together, this too will have its advantages for both of you. This may be a good match for Leo–Capricorn, even though the general trend isn't too promising.

LEO + AQUARIUS

Fire + Air = Hot Air

A relationship with an Aquarian can be wild, bizarre and anything but dull or uninteresting. You are opposite signs of the zodiac and therefore could attract each other, but will do so in strange ways that are difficult to understand.

Firstly, Aquarius is ruled by the unpredictable planet Uranus, which strongly indicates the unusual—if not outlandish—circumstance in which you bump into each other. There could be a lot of laughter, zaniness or just confusion associated with your coming together.

You operate from a heart level and speak your mind as it is. Aquarius does the same; however, they operate very much on an intellectual level and this may evoke some mistrust from you. But don't worry; they actually do believe in what they're saying.

The Aquarian is outspoken, wilful and revolutionary in nature. You admire their level of independence but still somehow find it hard to put your finger on what their true motivations are.

You need to spend time away from society, from the group, and really get to know your Aquarian on a one on one basis if you are to connect with them properly. Once you do this, you'll be pleased to note that there are indeed some facets of both your personalities that have a common meeting point.

By all means, consider a relationship with Aquarius, but only on the proviso that you're prepared to drop everything at a moment's notice and yield to their highly spirited and adventurous demands. They want you to prove to them that you're as courageous and committed to your ideals as they are, which may actually mean being as committed to their ideals as they are. In any case, you'll be making some fairly significant concessions if you want this relationship to be long-term.

And speaking of long-term relationships, Aquarians born between the 21st and 30th of January will entice you enough to warrant serious consideration. Certainly, there are basic differences between any Leo and Aquarian, but the positives may outweigh the negatives with Aquarians born during this period.

If you take note of an Aquarian born between the 31st of January and the 8th of February, you'll be taken by their friendly, open nature and their genuineness. They have plenty of experiences to share, which will intrigue and entice you into sharing some of those experiences with them. This is romantically a reasonably good combination as far as Leo and Aquarius are concerned.

Ranking Leo and Aquarius, the best match would have to be with those born between the 9th and the 19th of February. They have a supportive attitude and are not wholly and solely self-absorbed like some Aquarians. They are genuinely interested in what you want out of life and will work hard in compromising to ensure your needs are well taken care of, too.

LEO + PISCES
Fire + Water = Steam

Don't feel too bad if you can't quite figure out your Piscean partner. You're not alone in trying to fathom the depths of the spiritual and idealistic Neptunian temperament of those born under this rare and mystical sign.

Pisces is the twelfth sign of the zodiac, often considered to be the most spiritually evolved sign. They are concerned with sacrificing themselves for a higher ideal and this might be a little difficult for you to understand if you're not yet an evolved Leo.

If, on the other hand, you have climbed the ladder of the heights of evolution then you'll connect well with Pisces, whose ruling planets Neptune and Jupiter are reasonably friendly with your own ruler, the Sun. They are, however, a water sign so, having said all this, you need to bear in mind that they operate primarily from an emotional basis.

Pisces is moody, intuitive and often out of touch with the moment by moment practicality of things. You need them to be present with you in everything you're doing and this might make you feel ignored. That's not the case. Pisces is connected to you on a very different level and you may mistake this for absent-mindedness or disinterest. My recommendation is not to see it like this because in some ways, Pisces and Leo may actually work quite well. You can offer them direction in life and help them ground themselves here on planet Earth. You can help them develop self-confidence and, secretly, even if they don't say it to you directly, they admire your high level of confidence and exuberant personality. They will be proud to be associated with you.

However, don't expect fire and brimstone between the sheets in the bedroom when it comes to your sexual relationship with Pisces. Their approach to sex and the lustful side of life is again also very idealistic. They work from the inside out—remember that. If you're attuned to their inner vibration, their self-sacrificial attitudes and their desire to give at all costs, you may just start to understand where they're coming from and will yourself learn many things about the true nature of love.

Your relationship with Pisces born between the 20th and the 28th or 29th of February may not go that well. Once you overcome your initial sexual attraction, the fact of the matter is that this is not a particularly stable material combination and financial problems could plague your relationship.

You'll admire the sensitivity of Pisces born between the 1st and 10th of March, with this group being extremely responsive to your emotional and physical needs. You have a natural attraction to them and will also be elevated by their spiritual and imaginative discussions.

A Piscean born between the 11th and the 20th of March is a great match for you. They have considerably more fire than your typical Piscean because of their co-rulership by the sign of Scorpio. They have great sexual and passionate energy to express and are more than happy to share that with you, much to your satisfaction.

2010:
The Year Ahead

*Our plans miscarry because they have no aim. When a
man does not know what harbour he is making for,
no wind is the right wind.*

—Seneca

Romance and friendship

The powerful and energetic Mars dominates your
relationship landscape in the early part of 2010.
It ensures dynamic associations with others. You
will be aggressive about going after what you want
and will not be waiting around for what chance has
to offer you but rather will demand your personal,
emotional and sexual needs are fully met. This is
not the year to be a wallflower.

Lucky Jupiter spends the first month of the year
in your zone of marriage and love with idealistic
Neptune. You're dreamy about romance but must
keep your feet firmly planted on the ground. You
might find yourself experiencing your own fantasy
rather than the reality of the situation. You will have
a tendency to exaggerate your feelings. You can
meet someone who completely sweeps you off your
feet, so try to read between the lines before giving
your heart over to smooth talkers.

Mars moves into retrograde motion throughout
the first part of the year. In February it enters your
zone of secrets as well as hidden enemies. You must
be careful to keep your cards close to your chest and
not automatically believe that everyone you share
your heart with has your best interests in mind.
You could be disappointed to find that someone

you trust betrays you or lets you down. You might have some suspicions about the motives of others, so trust your intuition because it will be strong and most probably correct.

You're injury prone in February as well, but this may also relate to your emotions rather than your physical wellbeing. You are probably more sensitive than usual and the words of your spouse or partner may cut deeply. You feel vulnerable and unable to accept criticism—as constructive as it may be. Try to regard what others say with respect and don't take what is said to heart. It is in your best interests to improve yourself, and those who love you are more than likely concerned about you and want to help you.

During February you are attractive and could also catch the eye of someone as charming as yourself. But jealousy may prevail if this person gets the attention of others, too. It's up to you to look your best and lift up your standards to those of your partner or whomever you are attracted to. Don't let any negative emotions interfere with what could become a beautiful romantic interlude for you.

March is a most interesting time when your sexual energies will be very powerful. Mars will re-enter your Sun sign and Jupiter, the Sun, Venus and Uranus will present you with opportunities to explore the sensual and sexual elements of your relationships. This is also an opportune time to venture out, meet new people and explore areas that you've only ever dreamed of.

You are poetic, artistic and in love with cultural opportunities throughout April. The Sun, Mercury and Venus indicate a love of travel and higher education. It's possible that the people you meet at this time are more refined than you are. As a result, you will decide firmly to improve your internal awareness; that is, your understanding of others through psychology, meditation and philosophy.

This year you are interested in, and deeply committed to, transforming your relationships, which is shown by Jupiter moving through your eighth zone of personal and relationship transformation. You are idealistic and will want to reach for a bigger and better emotional frontier. If you're with someone who is as committed as you are to improving your relationship, then this will be a wonderful year in which you'll make great strides personally. There is the possibility, however, especially in May and June, that you could be out of sync with the one you love most.

Mars will re-enter its normal course creating a more demanding situation for you on the home front. Your personal affairs with relatives, your spouse or lover, will be difficult. You will be emotionally reactive to things that normally wouldn't bother you. You are extremely perceptive and want a better quality of life. If these demands are resisted then war could break out, figuratively speaking. Tact and diplomacy will be a test of strength for you, and remember that it is not so much what has to be said that will make a difference in your love life, but how you present it to the other person.

You will be dealing with the personal problems of a friend throughout June. Friendships do come into the spotlight at this point in time, but the health or mental state of a close friend will be of concern to you. You need to exercise patience and compassion to help them through this difficult period. Unfortunately you may be a little too close to the situation, which could impact adversely upon you and some of your other personal relationships as well.

Venus offers you a great deal of relief throughout July when it moves into your Sun sign. You'll feel much more attractive and won't be so aggravated by others, even if there is quite a bit of tension around you. You will also feel considerably luckier during this interval because of the influence of Jupiter on you as well. These two first-rate beneficial planets of the zodiac will certainly bring you a dose of fortune and a few of Cupid's arrows whizzing in your direction as well!

In late July to early August you must be careful not to let anger and frustration damage a relationship. Venus will enter into a close dance with Mars and Saturn and your communications may reflect a certain amount of passive aggression. Expressing how you feel will now be of particular importance. If you have been bottling up your feelings and not been able to talk about those areas in your relationship that are unsatisfactory, this could be a difficult point in time for you.

In August, relationships with siblings will be paramount. If you are estranged or have been separated from a loved one for some time, that person may enter the picture once again and whatever issues that have not been resolved previously will now have to be dealt with. Fortunately Jupiter ensures that you can come out of this with a sense of equality and fairness. Try to listen to the other person's point of view and don't superimpose your feelings on the situation. Most importantly of all, you'll be tested not to rehash the past but to live fully in the present. Try to look forward so your relationship can flourish.

In September you are highly passionate and want to enjoy life, by partying and exploring what is on offer in the club scene and any other social scenario that presents itself. You may even decide to celebrate just for the sake of being able to be in the company of others. You are bold and also active, mentally as well as physically. The combination of Venus and Neptune hints at the fact that someone of a spiritual nature may have some important information that has a bearing on your personal relationships. The indicators are that you should listen carefully to what is said as this will beneficially help you.

You will continue to deal with the responsibilities of your partner or a friend in October. Sharing the burden of their dilemma and emotional problems is an expression of your love for them. If you can't make the time, however, you will soon realise that they are not happy as a result and will probably blame you for the problems they have, at least in part. Make sure you are able to allocate a little bit of time to help your friends through their difficult transitions in this last part of the year.

In October and November your work is cut out for you on the home front. An exceedingly busy period is forecast, so don't leave yourself short on time. You are sure to have many family members and relatives demanding their pound of flesh in the form of attention from you. Activities domestically will range from personal discussions to completing housework and renovations. A family reunion for some Leo-born individuals is also quite likely within this period.

In the last month of the year your love affairs and creative impulses are again set to reach a crescendo. You may find yourself the recipient of several invitations and could even have a choice between two prospective lovers. This should bolster your ego because you will have the rare dilemma of possibly needing to choose between two people.

Work and money

You'll be supremely productive in your work during 2010. This is due to the presence of Mars in your Sun sign as the year commences. You have abundant physical energy and will not have any problem working the extra hours required to achieve your ambitions. However, try not to overestimate your abilities in January. There may be unexpected twists and turns in your work and financial situations.

Problems can be brought about by your impatience and inability to research your subject diligently. You may also have become blocked by others and will feel frustrated in your attempts to complete your work and move to the next level. Bear in mind that all of this has to do with your ego and not other people.

In February you'll come across to others as a much more assertive individual in your work. This isn't to say you aren't already held in high esteem, but during this month it's more likely you'll be able to get the support from others that you so desire. Mercury makes you more communicative and you'll click with co-workers rather than feeling thwarted in your attempts.

Set up more stable work relationships in the early part of the year, especially throughout February and March. Look to older people who are more experienced and can help you in a mentoring role to become better at what you do. Because Mars will remain in the vicinity of your Sun sign at least up until July, it will seem that pushing yourself to your limits may be the required path to take. At first you may not wish to take the advice of someone who knows better. However, 'more is not necessarily better' and this is one of the lessons you will learn throughout the coming twelve months. Try to balance everything you do and the results will be far more satisfying.

March is a particularly important time for you as far as your financial resources are concerned.

During this time interval you are likely to be preoccupied with banking or taxation matters due to the strong placement of the Sun and Jupiter with Venus. One quick way to make more money is to get your money to work for you. 'Working smarter rather than harder' will be your key phrase.

You are lucky in April when Venus and Mercury transit your zone of professional achievement. Your charming ways will win over your employers and your clients alike. Co-workers will be much more agreeable and so you get a lot done in half the time. Many born under Leo can expect promotions throughout this period.

Rely on friends to help open doors for you during this month as well. You may receive news of a new position and will be fortunate in any interview you attend. Have your facts ready and don't be afraid to speak your mind for fear that you may put someone out of joint. The interviewer will be amenable to you, and Venus moving through your zone of financial gains is an excellent omen, indicating that you are likely to achieve a better position with a higher salary.

A desire to transform your work is quashed in June and July. Working in a more low-key manner will give you an insight into what needs to be changed to make your current work circumstances more viable. If you happen to work at home and consider yourself a home-maker by profession, these transits are no less impacting upon your day-to-day routine. Take note of how your work is affecting your health and how your physical wellbeing may also be undermining your output.

Take care of legal matters throughout August. Read the fine print in your contracts and don't be afraid to ask questions before signing on the dotted line. You may feel intimidated if you are in the company of someone more powerful who is demanding you give them a quick decision. In doing so, you will 'put your foot in it', which is a way of saying you could find yourself in trouble. Hold your ground and take your documentation away with you to get proper legal advice if you are confused. Even if it means losing a coveted position, there's nothing worse than finding that you've signed your life away and can't get out of the commitment.

This period of the year will be a little bit frustrating for you due to the combination of Venus and Mars. Hard work may not be giving you the results you would like, but this will start to pan out for you by around the end of September and early October. At this time you may choose to do some work at home or in another quieter place where you can change the pace and get away from annoying factors, including people who may be irritating you.

When Mars enters your fifth zone of creativity in November, you will again be feeling great about what you do and can contribute significantly to the team effort. The year 2010 should indeed be a successful one in which your vitality and charm will win you praise and provide you with additional opportunities to increase your income.

Karma, luck and meditation

You are extremely lucky throughout 2010 and this is evidenced by the position of Jupiter and Mars; those lucky planets having a strong influence over your Sun sign as the year begins. Your past karma will bring you your just desserts in the form of better relationships and more money as well. You'll feel happy but your energy and drive may be a little too much for others to handle. Part of your spiritual lesson throughout this year will be to share your resources but also to be sensitive to how others wish to receive what you offer.

Marriage, engagements, relationships and other love matters are promising in February with Venus and the Sun in your marital sector. These lucky energies continue throughout March and your sexual energies are also fully primed and ready for action. You can enjoy yourself and feel fulfilled in your most intimate relationships.

With the Sun in your spiritual zone in April, metaphysical matters and meditation will afford you the opportunity to deepen your sense of self and connect with the higher powers of the universe. Develop your intuitive powers because you may be focusing too much on the outer world and the material benefits that you can achieve through your actions. Just remember that the inner forces of nature also have their own treasures to open up to you if you only take the time to tune into them.

Career matters are favoured in May and June and

additional benefits from work are likely to come your way. In June as well, you should expect an increase of cash and generous offers from friends. This again is karma coming back around, to give you a pat on the back for your past good deeds.

Jupiter enters a significant position in your horoscope in the very last few days of June. Throughout the remainder of the year your past karmic actions will start to pay off handsomely. You have the support of everyone around you and, would you believe, even strangers, too. You will be the recipient of generosity. Your mind will be cleansed of some bad habits. You'll be surprised to learn how easy it will be to discard unhelpful mental and emotional patterns from the past.

LEO

2010:

Month by Month
Predictions

Misfortunes often sharpen the genius.

—Ovid

Highlights of the month

Nothing can stop you this month and with the power of Mars you are likely to achieve much more than you usually do. Apart from the energy you exude to the world around you, you will also be taking steps to work out your inner world this month and set things right in your personal life. Between the 1st and the 5th you will spend considerable time re-evaluating your past behaviour and one of your main resolutions will be to improve things in your most personal relationships.

Communications are strong between the 6th and the 10th. You have the ability to get your point across, but try not to be too forceful and dominating because this can go against your best interests. On the 14th, when Saturn moves into its retrograde motion, you may find that others misunderstand what you have to say, so try to be lucid and explain yourself again if you have to.

A solar eclipse on the 15th is very powerful and relates to your work and the people around you in your professional activities. You may discover new skills through your association with different people in that environment. Enemies may come to the fore as well, however, so you need to be diplomatic and exercise skill in the way you handle these obstacles to professional success.

Pay special attention to contracts and other negotiations around the 16th. When Mercury moves into its forward motion, you will be excited about the prospects appearing in many areas of your life. A new job offer or some coveted position within your existing employment situation will go favourably for you.

An important transit occurs around the 18th when Jupiter moves to your zone of shared financial resources. It appears that much of your attention is on money this month, but sexual and deeper interpersonal issues may also be implicated in this transit, which only occurs once every twelve years. Talk about your feelings, share your insights, and don't be afraid to discuss financial matters with your spouse or partner if you feel you've received a raw deal. They will be amenable to what you have to say.

Social affairs and your love life are greatly improved between the 19th and the 25th. Put aside enough time to enjoy the lovely vibrations of Venus when it moves to your zone of marriage at this time.

Although you may feel pulled in several different directions at once, you'll make the right choice if you show your lover that you care and that your work and own individual needs are not put before them in the queue of your priorities.

Romance and friendship

January is a great month for meeting people, but the lunar eclipse on the 1st might also cause you to be a little fearful of the way you are perceived. This will be out of character for you because normally you are much more outgoing.

On the 2nd, you'll feel much better about expressing yourself and this also has to do with Mars giving you a great lift within yourself.

There could be some unforseen challenges in your relationship between the 6th and the 10th. Don't let your frustrations get the better of you.

Your desire for companionship is particularly strong after the 11th when you'll demand much more attention from your lover or spouse. More than likely this will kick-start your relationship if it's been floundering for some time.

Children also feature strongly in your home arena during this phase and, up until the 12th, you'll be actively involved in some of their pastimes, school projects and sports affairs.

You spend a lot of time cleaning up around the house and possibly after someone close to you, much to your dismay, around the 13th. Keeping a tidy house will be difficult and may interfere with your plans to do other things.

You'll be reconsidering some of your life's values under the solar eclipse of the 15th. You want to eliminate any type of sloppiness, bad habits or other inconsistencies in your relationship. Try not to come on too strongly, however, as this could backfire on you.

Journeys, travels and other educational contacts are strongly hinted at between the 23rd and the 25th. Laying low may be necessary after the 27th. Watch your health at this time and don't be scared to delegate tasks to relatives and family members.

The month finishes on a good tone but brings up issues with someone who doesn't like the fact that you are calling the shots. Avoid accidents on the 31st by planning ahead of time and confirming your engagements first.

Work and money

Financial distractions on the 2nd cause you to re-evaluate your course of action. Impulsive spending between the 5th and the 11th is unwise and may cause headaches for you and your partner.

Business associates are also less than support-ive, particularly between the 13th and the 15th. You'll be feeling hot under the collar, especially if someone is opposing your way of doing things. You must curb your impulsiveness and use discretion before going into battle.

You may have some secret fears associated with your work or some contractual or legal matters after the 21st. By the 23rd, you won't be able to contain yourself and your nervous tension will need some outlet, at least in terms of discussing your fears with your employer.

If you are selling, negotiating or involving yourself in any sort of contractual obligation, try not to let your fear show. Make your decisions by the 27th, after which time you may lose a valuable opportunity if you've been dragging your feet. Decisiveness wins the day.

Destiny dates

Positive: 3, 4, 5, 11, 12, 16, 18, 19, 20, 24, 25
Negative: 13, 14, 27, 31
Mixed: 1, 2, 6, 7, 8, 9, 10, 15, 21, 22, 23

Highlights of the month

For those of you who have landed yourself in a relationship, February will be very important in learning more about your partner. Once the gloss wears off the initial idealistic interplay with someone, it's time to get down to the hard work of getting to know the deeper aspects of their personality.

Between the 8th and the 14th, much of your attention will be on gaining further insights into your lover and where your relationship might take you. Venus, the Sun and Neptune create an incredible amount of energy and excitement about your emotional involvements. But try to be realistic; settle into the relationship in a way that doesn't disturb other aspects of your life. It may be some time before you accustom yourself to the brand new habits of another.

For those of you in existing relationships, your standards may be too high and you may feel some disappointment in the air at this time. Around the

11th this will be underpinned by your need for more flexibility, compassion and understanding. Someone you thought you knew will be acting in ways that are completely out of character and this could be difficult for you. Try not to react to every minor detail of their behaviour. Let things slide and you will find that it's not as bad as you are imagining.

Your creative juices are flowing and this can be highlighted by the combined influence of the Sun and Neptune. Between the 15th and the 17th some wonderful social and creative opportunities are likely to occur and it's simply a matter of being in the right place at the right time to take advantage of these wonderful celestial energies. You may become nervous if a chance does present itself. However, the old saying 'nothing ventured, nothing gained' could well be applicable to you during this interval of the year.

On the 18th, Venus and Jupiter provide you with ample opportunity to fulfil yourself socially and professionally. Don't blow it. If you have a friend nudging you to do something you normally wouldn't attempt, put aside your fear and go along for the thrill value, at least. It may not be exactly what turns you on, but life is to be experienced and this could be one of those times when you'll be glad you stepped outside the square to try something different.

Miscommunications can be avoided around the 27th if you do a little homework first. Telephone calls may be missed or others may not receive your messages or e-mails. Don't leave this to chance because the outcome could depend on vital information that you have to provide. You mustn't cut corners and instead follow up if need be, even if you feel as if you are being somewhat of a nuisance. Others will appreciate your diligence and attention to detail.

Romance and friendship

You must curb your anger throughout February, even if things aren't going as quickly as you would like them to, or to the plan you have in mind. Between the 2nd and the 5th, you will be sharp in your speech and may get someone offside. It's better to direct your thoughts towards love and positive thinking rather than pointing out others' faults.

On the 6th, 7th and 8th, a co-operative approach will help you get back on track. Try to discuss your inner emotional needs readily and, if necessary, get your children onside if you are a parent. A group or family get-together to discuss a cohesive plan of action will now be necessary.

You might be confused or erratic in your relationships between the 10th and the 12th. Neptune and Venus make you look at things using a more idealistic frame of mind. You could miss vital clues to another person's real intentions. Don't put others up on a pedestal because you are likely to be disappointed.

Deception is likely on the 13th and 14th, with the Moon conjoining Mercury. Trusting others with your valuables or possessions, especially if they have some sentimental value to you, is not advisable.

An extra dose of affection is likely around the 19th. When your sense of self is strong then others will feel entertained in your company. There are material benefits and tactical opportunities that arise through your social commitments and inter-actions, particularly from the 22nd to the 24th. Be seen and you will achieve much more than you expect.

A behind the scenes social encounter could be necessary due to some confrontation reaching a crescendo in your life. It's important not to blow things out of proportion between the 26th and the 28th. You are likely to be more reactive than normal, so listen with your intuition, not just your ears.

Work and money

Your mind is incredibly switched on this month and you'll be particularly interested in filing, organising your desk and getting rid of those mountains of paperwork that have become an eyesore. Between the 2nd and the 5th, you'll be able to achieve much more than usual, so take the phone off the hook and let your voicemail do the talking.

Investments are promising between the 7th and the 10th. Involve yourself with friends who under-stand speculative ventures and can give you a leg up. Get a taste of how your money can start to work for you.

Finances take a turn for the worse around the 14th when you realise you've overspent and not been frugal enough in the way you are enjoying your hard-earned money. This requires you to rethink your personal savings plan.

Keep your 'nose to the grindstone' between the 22nd and the 24th. There may be problems swirling around in your workplace, but you won't be inclined to involve yourself with any unpleasantness that may arise between third parties.

You have a strong drive to achieve your goals in the last few days of February, and some good news of a career nature may arrive on your desk by the 27th.

Destiny dates

Positive: 2, 3, 4, 5, 6, 7, 8, 9, 15, 16, 17, 18, 19
Negative: 26, 28
Mixed: 10, 11, 12, 13, 14, 22, 23, 24, 27

Highlights of the month

You are particularly inquisitive throughout March and between the 1st and the 5th may have your work cut out for you investigating and solving some problem. This may not necessarily be related to your work but it will most definitely occupy your mind and take up large slabs of your time.

There may be secrets you are dealing with this month—yours and those of others—and this could disturb you greatly if you don't look at the situation with a rational mind. You could make things worse than they are by imagining all sorts of grim outcomes. Get your facts right first before drawing your conclusions.

Your life improves greatly by the 7th when Venus enters your ninth zone of luck, education and travels. Put aside that special time with your lover, friend or spouse and travel with them; somewhere you can both be alone and truly give yourself the quality time that may have been missing for a while. It's an excellent opportunity to reconnect and re-establish the foundation of your relationship.

Educational matters are high on your agenda so many of you will be seriously investigating study courses, educational programmes and possibly even the odd lecture or workshop in which you can improve your creative skills and develop your pastimes and hobbies. Overall you'll feel expressive and happy, and will want to share these feelings with your friends and loved ones.

Dealing with publishing, writing, books and other forms of advertising and media will come to the fore between the 8th and the 11th. If you're planning to sell something, give some thought to the wording and the avenues from which you can get the best returns on your money. Letter writing will serve you well at this time. Jot down your thoughts and send memos, rather than relying on memory and hearsay, if what you have to say is important and might need to be referred to sometime in the future. This also has the added value of clarifying any misconceptions or disputes you could have ahead of you.

Between the 12th and the 16th you have a clearer idea of your agenda and Mars, which has been moving in reverse motion, moves back into its correct path to give you a boost physically and mentally. You will run into disputes with others who don't agree with your attitudes or decisions. You could lose a few friends; but stick to your guns, especially if you believe in what you're doing.

Try not to lose your cool between the 16th and

the 20th. Things could spin out of control so it's important to have a game plan and not let others distract you from what you wish to achieve. The Sun and Uranus will be responsible for some abrupt changes in plans.

The 21st to the 30th consolidates your desire for education and your communication should be back on track again at this time.

Romance and friendship

If you try to contain your feelings on the 1st, they might build up to such an unmanageable proportion that you're likely to say or do something you'll later regret. It's best to communicate your misgivings, even if this causes a backlash of sorts in your personal relationships.

Between the 6th and the 10th, you'll be engaged in many discussions but you'll feel as if you're just not quite good enough for the other person. You mustn't let old mental habits restrict you from growing, even if you feel vulnerable and possibly even shattered by what you hear. 'Keep a stiff upper lip', as they say.

New relationships are on the horizon after the 11th. This will be a perfect time to make decisions about your relationships overall. You are looking more deeply into the value of, and returns on, your emotional investments.

Between the 14th and the 16th, don't be afraid to reciprocate if you see that a friend or lover is not up to scratch in terms of their inner responses. You will demand what you need to make you feel happy.

The routine of your personal life is greatly disrupted after the 17th. You will have a desire to explore new avenues of love and friendship. Long journeys are on the cards and, especially between the 21st and the 23rd, you may venture on a trip somewhere to meet someone you've been corresponding with or met online, and this could be the commencement of an interesting relationship.

You will want to transform yourself and perform some sort of mental spring cleaning. 'Out with the old and in with the new' seems to be your key phrase between the 27th and the 31st. Your new year's resolution may kick in a little late; but, as they say, 'it's better late than never'.

Work and money

Money is particularly tight between the 2nd and the 4th and your mind may feel a little heavy with these financial responsibilities weighing upon your shoulders. Light relief is possible for you around the 8th when some work entertainment can help you forget these problems for a while.

Then, after the 14th, you could be the recipient of a will, legacy or some other endowment. Annuities, tax refunds or other savings you'd overlooked may help smooth over some of your financially difficult times.

Educational matters fare well between the 18th and the 21st. A mini holiday could be offered to you, but only in the form of lectures, extra-curricular studies or home study courses. A change is as good as a holiday, so I recommend you consider this opportunity and take a little bit of time out. You'll be able to 'kill two birds with one stone'.

Lost money or valuables that have been hidden for sometime may come to light between the 23rd and the 26th. Put this money or valuable item to good use. You may see that old habit of wastefulness rear its ugly head again. Keep a tight rein on your expenditure till the 31st.

Destiny dates

Positive: 5, 11, 18, 19, 20, 21, 22, 23, 24, 25, 26, 27, 28, 29, 30, 31

Negative: 8, 9, 10, 17

Mixed: 1, 2, 3, 4, 7, 12, 13, 14, 15, 16

Highlights of the month

This month is particularly important for you professionally, especially if you hold a position where you deal with the public. For others born under Leo it is still equally significant because your self-esteem and the way others perceive you will contribute to your future success in a big way.

Between the 1st and the 3rd you will be particularly attractive and what you have to share with others will be easily received without any contention. Your competitors will be powerless against you and employers and co-workers will be 100 per cent behind your plans and your ideas. There should be no stopping you during this period of the year. If you can attend interviews for a job promotion or an increase in salary, now is the time to do it. You should receive a positive response in every respect.

Important news can arrive after the 4th. You may have given up on some job prospects, or course of action, only to find that an out-of-the-blue favourable decision has been reached and the news of it will be a cause for celebration. This is also the time to negotiate new terms and conditions with your employer if you've not been particularly happy about your circumstances. Again, you can expect a positive outcome in your discussions.

Re-evaluating your financial circumstances is high on your agenda after the 7th. You may have to cut back on many of your expenses, but you will realise that this is the only way you can secure your future and put your mind at ease. If you want to look carefully at your banking and credit card statements, you'll be shocked at just how much you're spending on 'useless necessities', if I can explain them like that.

You'll be able to stretch a dollar much further during this cycle and will be pleased at the fact that you are making appropriate changes in the way you manage your money. Your partner or spouse will also be quite impressed at your ability to tighten your belt.

You mustn't promise what you can't deliver around the 18th, even if it seems someone above you has given you their approval to proceed on some matter. You could be tempted to give a subordinate or co-worker the green light only to learn later that the proverbial rug has been pulled out from under your feet by your superiors. Wait till you get their assurances in writing before giving others the so-called 'good news'.

After the 25th you can expect a friendship to deepen. Even if you thought you knew someone well, this is a time when the bonds between you and others can become stronger. If you need assistance in some area of your life, you can rely on friends this month.

Romance and friendship

You feel exciting, communicative and particularly attractive between the 1st and the 3rd. Venus and Mercury dominate the celestial landscape, making you charming and available. Previously you may have spent time in an emotional and social wilderness, probably because you've been trying to break some old habits.

The danger between the 4th and the 10th is that your social engagements may draw you back into circumstances that tempt you to reconnect with these old habits again. This could be smoking, alcohol or other recreational substance abuse. Be careful.

A close friend should be regarded as a mentor after the 15th. This person can offer you valuable advice that is practical as well as hard to come by. Don't let your ego get the better of you. You'll know in your heart of hearts that the advice being offered is absolutely useful and most timely.

Between the 17th and the 20th, your organisational skills could be called upon to help in a social function. Your level of concentration is well tuned and you will be dedicated to creating a successful event.

However, don't be afraid to delegate some of the

associated tasks if too much is being expected of you. Yes, you will want to please your friends; but to what extent are they prepared to please you in return, or help you to help them?

You may feel lazy or awkward between the 26th and the 28th. You have the opportunity to go on a blind date, only to get cold feet at the last minute. But go along for the social value anyway, if not for the romantic potential. You will more than likely have a great time.

The Moon transits your zone of love affairs on the 30th, indicating an emotionally fulfilling conclusion to the month.

Work and money

On the 7th, seize the opportunity to close a deal and don't be afraid to do it in a social context as well. Playing golf, lunching, wining and dining with your clients will pay handsome dividends. This is far superior to simply pulling out contracts and 'doing it by the book'.

All through this period, you're more likely to be direct, even arrogant in the way you speak the truth. This has its downside after the 15th, but at least people will know where they stand with you. You won't be prepared to waste excessive amounts of time on people who can't make the right decision, in your opinion. On to greener pastures!

Speed as well as accuracy will be a beautiful combination for you to achieve a professional objective around the 25th. Your creativity is unfettered when you have the go-ahead to do things in the way you feel will bring the quickest and most beneficial results for your business. There's a great deal of optimism showing here, which is coupled with your dynamic energy, indicating a successful close to the month of April.

Between the 28th and the 30th, tie up some loose ends associated with real estate, especially if you are interested in its commercial benefits at this time.

Destiny dates

Positive: 1, 2, 3, 17, 18, 19, 20, 25, 29, 30
Negative: 5, 6, 8, 9, 10, 26, 27
Mixed: 4, 7, 15, 28

Highlights of the month

You'll probably feel exhausted and need a rest this month. Expending so much energy does come at a price, doesn't it, Leo? Although you'll feel physically exhausted you'll still feel a considerable lift in your mental energies, especially between the 5th and the 12th.

Much of your attention is on legal and/or professional matters. You could reach a turning point in your profession, where your goals and aspirations need to be lined up with your heart's desire and the practical responsibilities with which you find yourself burdened.

As a result of these influences you may feel out of your element by the 15th, requiring a complete change of surroundings. If this is not possible you will feel unwell or generally out of sync with everyone around you.

By the 20th, when Venus moves to the quiet zone of your horoscope, it will be a great idea to take yourself out of the loop and spend time with friends in a more relaxed atmosphere. This will not be the result of a full-blown crisis, just one in which the stress and strains of everyday life need to be put aside while you recharge your batteries.

The Moon is in an excellent placement as the month commences and your emotional 'warmth' is at a much higher temperature at this time, so to speak. You will feel comfortable about expressing your feelings and some other important aspects of your relationship, which will help your partner to draw strength from you. This could come at a time when they are feeling the pressure in their own personal lives, so they will greatly appreciate your attention in helping them.

Between the 21st and the 25th you might feel disillusioned by the humdrum pace of your social situation and will need to take the initiative to stir up some more creative 'oomph' in your peer group. If you're hanging around people who are moaning and groaning about how bad life is, this will annoy you and you'll feel responsible for showing them alternative views of life. This could be your chance to shine as a guru to your friends.

Between the 28th and the 31st, additional career obligations weigh heavily upon your shoulders. However, no man (or woman) is an island unto themselves, as they say, so do ask for help, even if your ego makes you feel reluctant to do so.

Under these same transits, confusing circumstances over some financial dealing with a friend may clear up, thereby paving the way for improved feelings between you. However, you mustn't overlook a transgression, if that has occurred, because this will make you seem weak and lose the respect of others.

Romance and friendship

Unless you give, you won't receive. This is the law of the universe and it's pronounced, and evident, in your interactions between the 2nd and the 5th. Serve the one you love. Support your friends and watch the love and support rebound tenfold. Service is to be your key activity during this phase.

You will find yourself surrounded by a whole new group of friends, especially between the 12th and the 14th. You may be torn between sharing your time with two different groups. There will be a whole new series of opportunities to grow emotionally and mentally as a result of this. Don't let fear get in the way of discarding what is no longer of use to you. That means relationships as well, Leo.

Between the 20th and the 22nd, you may resist the requests of an old friend to resolve some past dispute. If you look at this carefully, you'll see that you've been harbouring feelings of resentment for sometime. You may not want to recommence your relationship with this person but there's no harm in burying the hatchet, clearing the air and moving forward with a clear conscience.

Family activities are high on the agenda on the 23rd and the 24th. Entertaining on the home front will be enjoyable but could also exasperate you. One menu is sufficient. If you try to please everyone with their individual tastes, you will run yourself into the ground. Be firm, be a gracious host or hostess, but let everyone know in no uncertain terms that they have to play by your rules.

An enjoyable heart-to-heart conversation with an older female relative or family friend on the 25th will inspire you and give you a taste of what's possible in this world. Learning about your past family genealogy will also be of considerable interest to you and may help put together the final pieces of the jigsaw puzzle of your life.

Work and money

Cutbacks on the work scene could leave you frustrated between the 1st and the 6th. Basic essentials such as copy paper, pens and other stationery supplies may be conspicuously missing. You'll have to be resourceful, that's for sure. Unfortunately, you won't have a say in this and will have to grin and bear it.

Dealing with bureaucracy will be annoying, especially if you need quick answers, around the 10th. Take photocopies of all of your important documents, particularly if they relate to such things as housing and land taxes.

Expect lengthy and deep discussions with employers or other authoritarian figures after the 20th. Approaching these meetings with a conservative bent of mind is superior. Peddling your own progressive brand of solutions will be met with suspicion, to say the least. Before you can command others, you must serve a little more. Remain humble and present your case in as traditional a manner as possible.

Gaining a clearer definition of a business plan with a friend is necessary before putting your money on the table. Harebrained schemes for getting rich quickly are not apprbopriate for you. The lure of making money without hard work is a fantasy. Don't be tempted.

Destiny dates

Positive: 7, 8, 9, 11, 12, 13, 14
Negative: 1, 21, 22, 28, 29, 30, 31
Mixed: 2, 3, 4, 5, 6, 10, 20, 23, 24, 25

Highlights of the month

You approach the middle of the year with a higher degree of self-balance and purposefulness. Jupiter, the planet of luck and benevolence, moves into your zone of higher learning and good fortune around the 6th. Much of what you do will be with a greater sense of ease and depth in every department of your life. The combination of Jupiter and Uranus does indicate an unexpected dose of luck, so be prepared for some fun, extra earnings, a win or the unexpected gift or two.

For the first time in the year Mars moves away from your Sun sign, also adding to the benefits of Jupiter by removing your impulsiveness and argumentativeness. Relationships should go much more smoothly after the 9th. Your focus will shift from personal relationships and friendships to making money.

There is a danger of feeling smugly confident with your savings and other financial gains. You mustn't turn a blind eye to unexpected bills and expenses. You might leave yourself short, even though you are experiencing a great deal of luck and cash flow. Frugality and resourcefulness should remain your key words throughout this period.

Others may not completely understand your work ethic this month because you are emotionally intense about getting your work done and gaining maximum leverage from it. This could bring out hidden parts of your personality that others haven't seen before and it may unsettle them. Try to assure them you haven't changed and that you are simply on a mission to secure your financial future. Around the 10th, when Mercury conjoins your zone of profits, these effects will be experienced to the maximum.

Money and friendships will be very strongly linked but by the same token power struggles are also likely to be associated with these relationships. The temptation to combine your business with pleasure may need to be sidestepped for the time being until you understand more about what is at stake. Around the 21st you realise that it is far better to forfeit some extra cash rather than lose a good friend.

You may have to leave a few plans hanging up in the air after the 25th. Call this selfishness but there are times when you need to give yourself the priority rather than your work. Interpret the demands of a loved one as a blessing in disguise if they expect you to be at home a little more. Leave the office early, particularly if there are no pressing deadlines and spend some quality time with those you love.

The lunar eclipse on the 26th highlights essentially that the quality of service in your work is more important than financial gain. Chasing the dollar may have to take second place to looking after the needs of your clients and co-workers.

Romance and friendship

Communications will set the trend this month and from the 1st till the 4th you'll be happy at how open your lover is with you. They may, however, reveal some aspect of the past that can be rather harrowing. If you want to foster more honesty in future, you'll have to bite your tongue and simply accept this.

Being flexible is very important after the 6th. You may have your timetable clearly set, only to find that a friend desperately needs you to be available for them. If you are too rigid, you'll be blamed for not being compassionate enough. 'Damned if you do, and damned if you don't!'

Unless your friendships are allowing you to move into a spiritual dimension, you may feel frustrated with the situation between the 10th and the 15th. You'll be looking for a higher standard in your friendships, and the routine habit of simply visiting the same old pub or club will start to lose its appeal. It's up to you to instigate change within your peer group at this time, even if you'll be challenged for doing so.

Taking up a good cause and linking that to your social engagements is quite likely between the 16th and 17th. Giving charitable donations or working for a community or social group seems attractive and will also give you the sense that you are doing more than just living. You will feel comfortable in this role and it could be the commencement of a whole new way of life for you.

Speaking of lifestyle, you have a desire to change the status quo between the 24th and the 28th. Being more creative and wanting to express more of yourself to others, you'll be likely to investigate a new fashion statement for your wardrobe, hairstyle, or possibly even cosmetic surgery.

Work and money

With Saturn moving through your zone of income, you'll be acutely aware of your new approach to handling finances. You will be much more serious and less frivolous with the way you spend your hard-earned cash.

Between the 1st and the 5th, your attention is on the detail of your accounting systems. Keeping a tighter rein on your money and expenses will be important to you.

Imagination underpins your professional activities between the 8th and the 14th. You have to step outside the square and try new things, especially in a competitive marketplace. Dare to be brilliant, dazzling if need be; but remember, too, that someone else could attach the tall poppy syndrome to your plans and cause the downfall of this scenario.

Enemies may try to undercut you between the 17th and the 20th. Be a step ahead of them and, if you hear rumours or hot gossip, don't make matters worse by retaliating or responding to these half-truths.

You may have a lapse in judgement after the 25th when you spend a little more money than you should, probably because you've had one drink too many.

Destiny dates

Positive: 1, 2, 3, 4, 8, 9, 24, 26, 27, 28
Negative: 18, 19, 20, 21
Mixed: 6, 10, 11, 12, 13, 14, 15, 17, 25

Highlights of the month

It's a good thing to question your own belief systems and this will happen to you in July, particularly around the 6th when Uranus, the planet of progressive thinking, does an about-face in your zone of philosophy and religion. The people you meet at this time will have a marked influence on your thinking and attitude to life in general.

You won't miss a trick during July and, as Mercury enters your Sun sign on the 10th, you'll even need to prove your intellectual prowess. Putting into practice what you've learned will be essential for moving forward in your life. Examinations, tests and other battles of will should be evident at this time.

Fortunately for Mercury, the element of humour is not absent and my suggestion above all else is that you laugh off the more serious sides of life because there's a likelihood that the people you associate with will be taking things far too seriously. They know what to do to superimpose their brand of negative thinking on anything new and the only way out of this situation is to be a step ahead of them with a joke. Don't worry if it goes over their heads for the time being; the main thing is that you keep your spirits high and don't be subjected to the negative influences of other people.

You will have a desire to rummage through your belongings, memorabilia and past photographs to recollect some happy and not so happy memories. This will also trigger your desire to make contact with some old friends and possibly even lovers. School reunions and other get-togethers are not out of the question, so don't be surprised to receive a call after the 17th to be part of an event of this nature.

Saturn augments your concentration powers after the 21st and moves through your zone of contracts and direct communications. Interaction with your neighbours may not go smoothly and mediation may even be necessary to solve an ongoing problem with them. If you've had a belly full of their late-night parties, banging on doors and other irritating behaviour, this is the month you will say 'enough is enough!'.

Your confidence is extremely high after the 23rd when the Sun returns to the sign of Leo. Your best qualities will be available for the world to see and it's time for you to take centre stage once again. This is the commencement of a new yearly solar cycle, so make the most of it. Get out your best outfit, your best suit and tie, and spend a little money beautifying yourself to make a lasting impression. If you're on the prowl for love, your energy is perfectly suited to attracting the right mate during this period. Venus makes you particularly charming and alluring to potential partners.

Romance and friendship

Between the 1st and the 4th, what you see can't hurt you—or can it? You need to learn from your past mistakes to avoid making those mistakes again. With Mercury and the Sun passing through your zone of endings, hidden enemies and other secrets, you'll be pulling aside the curtain that is keeping part of your life in a state of mystery.

The period of the 8th to the 12th is extremely busy. However, your communication skills should have the edge and, if you're in some sort of friendly debate, you will come out the winner. Just be a little careful not to let idle chit-chat erode your valuable time. You've probably got better things to do and may only discover this after it's too late.

Around the 18th or 19th, your impatience could get the better of you. Unruly neighbours, demanding siblings, or friends who have little respect for you will cause you to blow up. You'll be banging heads at this time and so confrontations with these people and others could alienate you and create further tension in your life.

Between the 20th and the 23rd, you should take things one step at a time. Don't expect others to understand what you want from them if you haven't clearly defined what's on your mind. Be absolutely clear about your intentions and you'll avoid plenty of arguments during this rather frustrating phase of Mars and Saturn.

After the 24th you may try to overcompensate by going too far. Making an impression needn't require so much effort on your part. With Venus still positively influencing you, let the power of your charm do all the persuading.

Between the 26th and the 31st, you need to balance your passions, emotions and self-interests. You could be lowering your standards and settling for much less than you should. This applies equally to singles as to those who are in committed, long-term relationships.

Work and money

With Mars and Saturn powerfully influencing your financial zone, you could be in for a rough ride throughout the early part of July.

Between the 3rd and the 6th, take the time to read over contracts and don't rush things. Someone may be pushing you to make a decision against your better judgement. You could feel cornered. However, remember that the ball is in your court and you can return the serve when it pleases you, not others.

The peak of your financial concerns may occur between the 14th and the 16th. Don't avoid speaking to someone for fear that things could get out of control. You need clarification more than anything this month, and by the 17th you'll feel free of the problems we've just discussed here.

You don't always have to do everything for money and you'll realise this by the 22nd. Creative expression is its own reward. Don't expect financial remuneration for extra hours you put in on the job.

Your intellectual abilities will promote co-operation and joint investigation in your workplace on the 26th. A problem may have been overlooked by others. It will be up to you to draw some radical conclusions.

An additional piece of vital information is made available to you by the 28th.

Destiny dates

Positive: 8, 9, 10, 11, 12

Negative: 1, 2, 3, 4, 5, 14, 15, 16, 18, 19, 20, 24, 27, 29, 30, 31

Mixed: 6, 21, 22, 23, 26, 28

Highlights of the month

You have the golden touch this month and with Mercury and Venus both activating your financial sector you can feel confident you have enough money to enjoy life the way you want. You mustn't let Mars and Saturn spoil your good time, however. You could be lured into a sense of frustration by focusing on past mistakes, hurts and other negative memories, but don't go there.

Your mind is your best friend or your worst enemy and this will become crystal clear to you this month when you walk the tightrope between great joy and great disappointment. Hang in there until the 9th. You'll be able to resolve these contrary inner feelings.

You will tend to be more generous than usual and this is going to be highlighted after the 17th. In the past you've probably ignored cries for help from third world countries, self-help groups or other medical institutions trying to do research work to assist the downtrodden or those less fortunate than yourself. You could feel guilty about it and will want to extend your hand in a gesture of goodwill. Learning about other cultures and spiritual activities associated with them will be appealing.

Tensions in your environment need not immobilise you if you use these forces wisely. You may not feel quite as open with your partner or friends as you usually are. You could feel cool and detached in your manner; but you mustn't make any apologies for this and just accept that the cycles of the planets cause you to be sometimes up, sometimes down.

You can make this mood work to your advantage between the 18th and the 21st. If you need to discuss the direction of your love life openly, do so before the 21st when Mercury goes retrograde and your discussions could end up going round in circles. Be firm in asking for the respect you want.

Your passions run high after the 22nd when Venus and Mars conjoin in your third house of creative communication. It's a well-known fact that this third zone of your horoscope also has an influence on your musical tastes. Dancing, theatrical playacting and even gymnastics or physical sports that have a touch of the aesthetic in them will be at the forefront of some of your activities. If you have children or are involved in these areas, you could take a more active role in helping them and being part of their routine. This should be a pleasurable close to the month.

Romance and friendship

Issues of emotional control will damage your relationship now if you don't take a different approach. Between the 5th and the 7th, it's what's *not* said that will be vital. You'll find yourself in some twisted mind games with friends and lovers; but by the 9th you'll be in a better position to play your hand to make your true intentions known as well as extract the true motivations of others.

You feel a great deal of loyalty and trust towards someone, but by the 13th feel as if it's time to test them to see whether or not they can pass your emotional examination. Diplomacy will give you the edge but sadly you will find that they fail miserably. Don't feel badly about it, though, because you're probably giving more than you're receiving in that friendship, anyway.

An opportunity presented between the 20th and the 22nd will be unconventional, even somewhat outlandish, but this will be a perfect balance to the stressful Venus, Mars and Saturn combination in the heavens. You may be feeling cool or aloof in your existing relationship and need time out to explore other possibilities.

Your impulses are strong between the 23rd and the 27th. You could fall madly in love with some stranger and this will be because they are particularly sexually magnetic. This is an emotional and passionate time when you may not be thinking so clearly with your head; but boy, it could be a lot of fun!

You are lucky in love this month but may also be burdened by financial concerns or some additional domestic responsibilities. This will upset you and make you feel as if you're unable to give as much as you'd like. This could intensify between the 27th and the 30th.

Work and money

You should be thankful for any small benefits that present themselves to you this month. For example, there may be an increase in your salary but you may begrudge it, feeling you're worth more. However, on the 2nd, if your attitude is one of ingratitude, you may find yourself being short-changed next time around, too, when additional bonuses are made available. Be appreciative of any increases that come your way, regardless of their size.

By the 13th, you may realise fully that your workplace safety and health issues have not been up to scratch. You mustn't sweep this under the rug because there could be some dangerous consequences. Faulty power points, poor lighting, lack of ventilation or air conditioning can all contribute to declining health and future disease. Take the appropriate measures to rectify these issues, even though it may cut into your time and require more effort on your part.

'Despise the free lunch' on the 22nd. What might seem to be a boon may actually be a burden and later weigh you down. In fact, someone is out to get something from you, not necessarily give you something. You'll be clearer on this by the 27th and may do an about-face on a business alliance.

Destiny dates

Positive: 9, 13, 17, 23, 24, 25, 26
Negative: 2, 5, 6, 7, 18, 19
Mixed: 20, 21, 22, 27, 28, 29, 30

SEPTEMBER

Highlights of the month

Even if you are a female born under the sign of Leo, you'll be surprised at the number of women coming in and out of your life this month. The Moon now assumes an important role in your zone of career so you can expect more discussions and close working relationships with women. These forces emerge partly after the 9th and will work in your favour.

Family matters also occupy much of your attention after the 12th. Real estate prospects and getting your house in order will be your primary focus. Children, elderly parents and other relatives who have special needs now play an important part in your life. A deeper understanding of your relationship to them will emerge and this can be a mini-enlightenment of sorts. You may not have the time to spend on yourself or your social affairs but you can expect other socialising on home turf to make up for it.

Relationships heat up on the home front between the 15th and the 19th. Consensus is the important word in this time frame. Someone in your family, perhaps yourself, decides to move forward on a game plan without consulting others in the group. This tactic will fail even if you have the best of intentions. Before committing money to a project, make sure you get the go-ahead from all the people affected, even if they don't have any financial input. Anything from a paint job to a major renovation could have disastrous consequences for your relationships if others don't feel as if they've had a say in the matter.

It may be time to overhaul your vehicle, or get a service done. If you're finding it hard to stretch your dollar, you may need to ask for a loan or some credit. Don't overextend yourself but by the same token don't postpone the inevitable. Cars can also get sick, which could end up costing you much more money in the long run. Between the 19th and the 22nd take the time to book in your vehicle or other working machinery for a long-overdue service.

Several short journeys are forecast after the 23rd. They may not necessarily be of a pleasant nature and in some ways there is an element of responsibility attached to a trip. If you have relatives at a distance who need your assistance, connecting with them may be unavoidable at this time. However, it is not a bad idea to clarify the benefits of any such journeys beforehand.

Even if you know it's going to be a tough time,

it would be wise to get an idea of just how difficult it could be. Some careful planning can minimise a poor outcome. Your key phrase for the last week of September is damage control.

Romance and friendship

Making last-minute changes to your family routine will be irritating between the 1st and the 4th. You'll need to fit in these responsibilities creatively with other activities. Unfortunately, you have to bear some of the friction from others who have alternative plans to yours. Stick to your guns and the pleasure will be worth it.

Between the 6th and the 9th you have to succumb to your partner and say yes for the sake of peace. You will be feeling stressed or dominated, but by disagreeing and trying to have things go your way you'll only create more problems. Be agreeable and resolve the dilemma.

Planetary forces affect your love affairs between the 12th and the 14th and this could create indecision within you. If your love life is not working, it's probably because you have a pre-conditioned idea about these issues. Someone you meet now may have a different angle and will help you out of your stale state.

Between the 16th and the 22nd, try to figure out what's truly good or bad for you. You need to be prepared to take a punt and try something different in your existence. Nothing ventured, nothing gained.

You'll be over-taxing yourself emotionally between the 24th and the 26th. You need to weigh up the long-term costs and effectively balance the output of your energies. Stop trying to impress too many people for fear of not winning their approval. Just state your case, relax, and let it go.

There are some important planetary combinations influencing your social sphere between the 28th and the 30th. This is great news for your friendships and the fulfilment of one or two of your dreams. But don't let this distract you from your other obligations. Balance your social and personal needs.

Work and money

Continue monitoring your finances between the 3rd and the 6th. Due diligence and a concentrated effort on your part will help sort out some of the confusion you might have about money matters. Don't accept the first plan that's offered before you make a reasoned decision. Compare all of what's available first.

Between the 9th and the 14th, there'll be a tug of war within your heart. What you have may not seem enough and dissatisfaction will cause you to make premature judgements based on a knee jerk reaction. There is no harm in taking a second look at what's available in the workplace and not jumping to conclusions.

A legal matter may bother you on the 18th. You've overlooked a commitment, even though it was only verbal. Don't feel challenged by people threatening you at this time because it is just a ploy to weaken you and get you to agree to do things against your will.

You'll be confronted by a mountain of work between the 21st and the 25th. You need to be aware of what's coming and, if you're drowning yourself in paperwork, you may be losing sight of the bigger picture. Don't get too absorbed in the finer detail.

Destiny dates

Positive: 5, 28, 29, 30
Negative: 1, 2, 7, 8, 10, 11, 15, 23, 24, 25, 26
Mixed: 3, 4, 6, 9, 12, 13, 14, 16, 17, 18, 19, 20, 21, 22

Highlights of the month

This is a busy month. What you have to do may not feel comfortable and you prefer to hide away from the world for a while. Unfortunately that's not going to work and, with the Sun combining with Saturn in your zone of communications around the 1st, you have to stand up and tackle your problems head on. In addition, others may not be so accommodating to your needs and you'll be tested in your social skills and diplomacy.

My prediction is you'll pass through this time with flying colours, as long as you don't react too strongly to others' judgements of you. They may have a misconception of who you are and what your motivations might be. This is a common problem but here you will be one step ahead of the crowd.

You'll be asked to help solve some riddle or problem this month, as evidenced by Mercury moving through your zone of thinking. The task may be a difficult one but you'll be up to it after the 5th, so accept the challenge. This may be one of those periods when the pay-off is not necessarily monetary but your good name will be enhanced as a result and your reputation can grow. Over and above this, you'll enjoy the challenge of resolving an issue to both your own and any other's satisfaction.

If you're involved in sales or public speaking, then when touring, teaching or in any other sort of negotiation, you'll be extremely clear and articulate in the way you present your case. Sales agents will be lucky enough to earn better commissions and longer-term contracts. Your journeys will also be fruitful and you mustn't complain if your work or a client expects you to travel further than you would normally expect to. You'll gain extra unasked-for benefits.

Studying for your work is also on the cards throughout October and, although you'll have to put in some extra hours to learn the topics, it will no doubt help you develop greater skills that you can apply in your workplace now or in some future employment. Educational matters are spotlighted between the 21st and the 23rd.

If you're sitting through examinations or something like them, you'll be ready to take the test by the 28th when your mind and power of concentration will be supercharged. I expect you to come out on top with excellent results, irrespective of the arena in which you are being tested.

Romance and friendship

You may be desperate to improve your social status between the 4th and the 6th, but you mustn't appear to be trying too hard. Understand that the planets will give you the emotional support you need. One point, however: During this cycle, you mustn't take friendships for granted. People can only bear so much and remember that giving as well as taking is part and parcel of true friendship.

The period of the 8th to the 12th will bring you considerable sexual tension and/or excitement in your relationships. Working on your boundaries will be a fairly important component of how well your relationships work. If something doesn't feel right, draw a line in the sand.

Between the 13th and the 15th, you can smooth over many of your tensions and your lover will now be more agreeable. You're also likely to be unconditional in the way you express your love.

While this is one of the major secrets of a fulfilling love life, my strong suggestion for you between the 16th and the 19th is that you now keep a thorough control over any highly passionate impulses. You may need to keep your cards a little closer to your chest rather than speaking openly about what you want. This will give you a strategic edge in your relationships. 'Silence is golden' and gives you the upper hand.

There are some unexpected events domestically between the 23rd and the 29th. Someone in your

family circle may get up and leave quite unexpect-
edly. If you're a parent with children in their late
teens or early twenties, you may need to talk some
sense into them before they throw all cares to the
wind.

Work and money

Between the 3rd and the 9th you have to be beyond
reproach if you're going to lecture others. Your
personal habits and belief systems could come
into question if you're expecting others to behave
in a certain way. This is one case where the statement 'do as I say and not as I do' is an inadequate
argument.

You could be caught off guard if you're looking
at investing and overhauling your finances between
the 11th and the 15th. You mustn't listen to the
layperson who is a supposed 'expert'. Because
you yourself haven't got the requisite knowledge,
you might assume that their jargon is a reflection
of some deeper wisdom, which isn't necessarily
the case.

You'll be excited to learn about some new
methods to 'up the ante' with your earnings, but
please be careful of treading on the toes of others
when doing so. It's fine being all fired up about
sharing your vision of wealth and success with your
friends but, if you overdo it, you could start to annoy
them.

I see considerable extravagance around you
after the 28th. There's no use spending all your

hard-earned cash only to find yourself back to square one economically. Continue to be moderate in your spending and don't throw bad money after good simply to make an impression on others.

Destiny dates

Positive: 21, 22

Negative: 12, 24, 25, 26, 27, 29

Mixed: 3, 4, 5, 6, 7, 8, 9, 10, 11, 13, 14, 15, 16, 17, 18, 19, 23, 28

Highlights of the month

Your mind could be off with the fairies, so to speak, in the first few days of the month, so try to pay more attention to what other people are saying otherwise you'll miss some crucial advice or direction.

During the period of the 1st till the 4th you may be invited somewhere only to find yourself lost on the way. Allow additional time to study your directory or better still get yourself a satellite navigation system in your car. They're not that expensive and will save you a lot of time, especially if you've got a somewhat poor sense of direction.

Nervous tension to do with your savings, taxes and other investment portfolios will cause you to lose sleep and be distracted from other important work this month. Speculations after the 9th are likely to be done in haste and this is ill-advised. You may be listening to the wrong people when it comes to making a quick buck. Remember that unless you carefully analyse the markets and study business and investments diligently, you are as good as gambling.

Jupiter's combination with Uranus can throw a spanner in the works with a surprise announcement by your spouse or a business partner around the 19th or 20th. It is far preferable to have your own bank account than rely on other people's financial arrangements. If you're at the mercy of what's happening somewhere else, you'll never be totally financially independent. Now is the time to turn that around. Make some decisive steps towards taking full control of your own financial situation.

If a plan backfires now, you've only got yourself to blame. You may have been taking your eye off the ball, while others have been running with it. Why would you then be surprised if the rules of engagement change as well? Still, you do have a say, and probably have a little more control than you think you do.

If some of these issues are still lingering from a domestic fallout several months earlier, your negotiation skills will require a reasonable amount of sweetener to make the cup palatable to others. Try to be nice when demanding what you believe is a fair deal for all concerned. It may just work for you.

If your children are at an age where they are likely to want freedom and independence because they are adults, this is a time where one of them may leave your domestic situation. What is known as the empty nest syndrome could now be encountered and needs to be dealt with.

Between the 28th and the 30th, take the time to talk to your children about their plans so that you're not completely bowled over when, out of the blue, they decide to pack their bags and leave.

Romance and friendship

There may be irritating social obligations between the 4th and the 8th. Someone might put the hard word on you and you'll have no choice but to sacrifice your time, energy and—hopefully not money—to fulfil their demands.

From the 9th till the 13th, friendship and love are spotlighted and will give you considerable satisfaction. Because of the presence of Venus, your physical looks and charm will play an increasingly larger role in attracting all sorts of people to you. Don't let your ego get the better of you, but of course it's okay to soak up just a little bit of adulation.

Expect lots of fun times and enjoyable pastimes from the 14th to the 20th. You'll find yourself in the company of those who are like-minded. It's also a cycle in which your artistic endeavours will prosper and, should you choose to take up some sort of artistic or creative activity, you'll feel very comfortable channelling your energies.

From the 22nd to the 24th there's a wonderful opportunity for you to hook up with an unusual group of people in some sort of social event that is not a run-of-the-mill situation. If this is apart from your usual peer group, it's probably best to keep the details of it a secret or you may be ridiculed for trying something so different.

Travel urges are growing from the 25th to the 29th, so it's not a bad time to get out your brochures and make some firm plans. Someone from a foreign place could befriend you and this could trigger your interest in different cultures.

Around the 30th exciting affairs could eventuate and you need to seize the opportunity quickly enough, otherwise you could regret having been too slow off the mark.

Work and money

It's a great feeling, having the appreciation and respect of those you work with and for. This is most likely your experience between the 1st and the 5th because your mental brilliance will captivate the imagination of others. They will feel inspired by you, which gives you the opportunity to prove your abilities as a leader, even if it's only a temporary position.

Networking your skills provides many opportunities in your career between the 10th and the 19th. Some gathering or a social event may be a key to opening new doors in your professional life. Dress to the max and put your best foot forward.

Decisions that have been hanging in limbo can move forward after the 12th. Having the correct facts at your fingertips helps communications. You have more confidence to speak your mind, knowing that you can back up what you say with the correct data.

A comfortable period at work awaits you between the 20th and the 24th. A get-together with co-workers and family members to show your successes of the year is likely, and this should be a special time where connections between work and family are harmonious.

Destiny dates

Positive: 9, 10, 11, 12, 13, 14, 15, 16, 17, 18, 21, 22, 23, 24, 25, 26, 27

Negative: 6, 7, 8

Mixed: 1, 2, 3, 4, 5, 19, 20, 28, 29, 30

Highlights of the month

In this last month of the year, you would think that fun, Christmas cheer and other festive activities would dominate your life, wouldn't you, but this couldn't be further from the truth. In fact, there may be more work around than you had anticipated, so clear the decks and be prepared to roll up your sleeves and get into it, at least until the 10th. You may have no choice because several of your work colleagues may decide to disappear early, leaving you to shoulder the additional workload.

Mercury's retrogression late in the year indicates you might have overlooked a few jobs or deadlines only to find that you're having to play catch-up between the 12th and the 18th. Part of the problem may have been your interpretation of the directions given to you by your manager. Slacking off will not exclude you from the extra hours you will have to put in now to level the playing field. There's no use ignoring the prevailing issue or trying to postpone fixing it till after Christmas. You'll only feel irritated and won't enjoy your Christmas dinner. My advice is: better to do it now and get it out of the way.

You should expect at least one blow up prior to Christmas Day and the most likely timing of that—from what I see in your horoscope—is the period of the 14th till the 19th, when Mercury and Pluto conjoin. You could be grilled by someone who has no real authority and you could retaliate, creating some bad blood in the process. Work could be a sensitive issue and the people you're dealing with may be just as strung out as you are. Try to remain empathetic about this fact and no harm will come to you.

Watch your health around the 20th, leading up to Christmas. Don't go rushing headlong into things; give yourself ample time and, if you are unclear about the way to do something, don't be too proud to ask for assistance. You're likely to hurt yourself or possibly damage some apparatus, computer technology or other machinery. Read the instructions!

There is a final lunar eclipse on the 21st of December, which takes place in your zone of friend-ships. This is the final movement in the Leo forecast for 2010 and it hints at the fact that much of your satisfaction in the last couple of weeks of the year will hinge upon the successful communication you will have with friends. As burdened as you will now be by your workload, accommodate a friend's call for help. It won't erode too much of your own valuable time but it will go a long way towards cementing your bonds of friendship with this person.

Romance and friendship

From the 2nd to the 5th, don't let your high level of energy cause unexpected mishaps or injuries. It's best to move a little more slowly and think about your actions before you begin them.

From the 7th to the 10th, your long-term romantic plans may have to be postponed and this might be upsetting, especially if you'd looked forward to an engagement or even a wedding date. However, don't let these turn of events throw your life into chaos. There will be a good reason for what's happening: the universe has a mind of its own and you will benefit from working harmoniously with this idea. Keep an open, positive mind that things will work out for the better.

Between the 16th and the 19th, an unusual situation arising with a friendship might start to lead to feelings of romance. This may be particularly tricky if you happen to work with this individual. The situation could be confusing when, after having developed an attitude of professionalism together, you find you now have a much deeper sense of connectedness with them. Explore the relationship by all means, but don't let it ruin your workplace ethics.

Your sports and physical pastimes are high on the agenda between the 20th and the 25th. This is a time to explore new hobbies and outdoor activities with which you can combine your social life. Don't forget the added benefit of renewing your health and re-invigorating your mental and emotional faculties.

The period of the 28th till the 30th could be a testing cycle for you when your philosophy, religion or belief systems will be put to the test. You need to prove that you have the courage of your convictions or people may consider you to be the great pretender. You'll be thoroughly scrutinised by your peers, so it's better to say as little as possible.

Work and money

Pay more attention to your letter writing skills and the means by which you communicate between the 1st and the 4th. Communication devices may need to be tested thoroughly, possibly even upgraded. Use your perks at work to save yourself money by putting it on the professional bill.

A desire to improve your lifestyle may force you to reconsider some of your financial obligations and whether or not you can afford such a change. Industry and consumer magazines can be helpful in this respect and will give you good comparisons based upon price and quality. This is likely to be strongly highlighted between the 12th and the 18th.

Focus your attention on something that's unique after the 20th; something that reflects who you really are as a person. Don't be scared to work hard to get a plan up and running and then stick to it, irrespective of what others might think. Of course, keep it light-hearted and don't forget to add a touch of humour to everything you do leading up to Christmas.

Courage and earnestness are the key words after the 23rd. Use grit and determination to make some valuable contributions to your workplace and your community. Social work, donations and other charitable activities have karmic financial benefits.

Destiny dates

Positive: 21, 22, 23, 24, 25
Negative: 1, 2, 3, 4, 5, 7, 8, 9, 10, 28, 29, 30
Mixed: 12, 13, 14, 15, 16, 17, 18, 19, 20

LEO

2010:
Astronumerology

*Times of great calamity and confusion have ever been
productive of the greatest minds. The purest ore is
produced from the hottest furnace, and the brightest
thunderbolt is elicited from the darkest storm.*

—Charles Caleb Colton

The power behind your name

By adding the numbers of your name you can see
which planet is ruling you. Each of the letters of
the alphabet is assigned a number, which is listed
below. These numbers are ruled by the planets.
This is according to the ancient Chaldean system of
numerology and is very different to the Pythagorean
system to which many refer.

Each number is assigned a planet:

AIQJY	=	1	**Sun**
BKR	=	2	**Moon**
CGLS	=	3	**Jupiter**
DMT	=	4	**Uranus**
EHNX	=	5	**Mercury**
UVW	=	6	**Venus**
OZ	=	7	**Neptune**
FP	=	8	**Saturn**
—	=	9	**Mars**

Notice that the number 9 is not aligned with a letter because it is considered special. Once the numbers have been added you will see that a single planet rules your name and personal affairs. Many famous actors, writers and musicians change their names to attract the energy of a luckier planet. You can experiment with the list and try new names or add the letters of your second name to see how that vibration suits you. It's a lot of fun!

Here is an example of how to find out the power of your name. If your name is John Smith, calculate the ruling planet by assigning each letter to a number in the table like this:

J O H N S M I T H
1 7 5 5 3 4 1 4 5

Now add the numbers like this:
1 + 7 + 5 + 5 + 3 + 4 + 1 + 4 + 5 = 35
Then add 3 + 5 = 8

The ruling number of John Smith's name is 8, which is ruled by Saturn. Now study the name-number table to reveal the power of your name. The numbers 3 and 5 will also play a secondary role in John's character and destiny, so in this case you would also study the effects of Jupiter and Mercury.

Name-number table

Your name number	Ruling planet	Your name characteristics
1	**Sun**	Magnetic individual. Great energy and life force. Physically dynamic and sociable. Attracts good friends and individuals in powerful positions. Good government connections. Intelligent, impressive, flashy and victorious. A loyal number for relationships.
2	**Moon**	Soft, emotional nature. Changeable moods but psychic, intuitive senses. Imaginative nature and empathetic expression of feelings. Loves family, mother and home life. Night owl who probably needs more sleep. Success with the public and/or women.
3	**Jupiter**	Outgoing, optimistic number with lucky overtones. Attracts opportunities without trying. Good sense of timing. Religious or spiritual aspirations.

Your name number	Ruling planet	Your name characteristics
		Can investigate the meaning of life. Loves to travel and explore the world and people.
4	Uranus	Explosive character with many unusual aspects. Likes the untried and novel. Forward thinking, with many extraordinary friends. Gets fed up easily so needs plenty of invigorating experiences. Pioneering, technological and imaginative. Wilful and stubborn when wants to be. Unexpected events in life may be positive or negative.
5	Mercury	Quick-thinking mind with great powers of speech. Extremely vigorous life; always on the go and lives on nervous energy. Youthful attitude and never grows old. Looks younger than actual age. Young friends and humorous disposition. Loves reading and writing.
6	Venus	Delightful personality. Graceful and attractive character who cherishes friends

Your name number	Ruling planet	Your name characteristics
		and social life. Musical or artistic interests. Good for money making as well as abundant love affairs. Career in the public eye is possible. Loves family but is often overly concerned by friends.
7	**Neptune**	Intuitive, spiritual and self-sacrificing nature. Easily misled by those who need help. Loves to dream of life's possibilities. Has curative powers. Dreams are revealing and prophetic. Loves the water and will have many journeys in life. Spiritual aspirations dominate worldly desires.
8	**Saturn**	Hard-working, focused individual with slow but certain success. Incredible concentration and self-sacrifice for a goal.
		Money orientated but generous when trust is gained. Professional but may be a hard taskmaster. Demands

| | | highest standards and needs to learn to enjoy life a little more. |
| 9 | **Mars** | Fantastic physical drive and ambition. Sports and outdoor activities are keys to wellbeing. Confrontational. Likes to work and play just as hard. Caring and protective of family, friends and territory. Individual tastes in life but is also self-absorbed. Needs to listen to others' advice to gain greater success. |

Your 2010 planetary ruler

Astrology and numerology are very intimately connected. As already shown, each planet rules over a number between 1 and 9. Both your name *and* your birth date are ruled by planetary energies.

Add the numbers of your birth date and the year in question to find out which planet will control the coming year for you.

For example, if you were born on the 12th of November, add the numerals 1 and 2 (12, your day of birth) and 1 and 1 (11, your month of birth) to the year in question, in this case 2010 (the current year), like this:

1 + 2 + 1 + 1 + 2 + 0 + 1 + 0 = 8

The planet ruling your individual karma for 2010 will be Saturn because this planet rules the number 8.

You can even take your ruling name-number as shown earlier and add it to the year in question to throw more light on your coming personal affairs, like this:

John Smith = 8

Year coming = 2010

8 + 2 + 0 + 1 + 0 = 11

1 + 1 = 2

Therefore, 2 is the ruling number of the combined name and date vibrations. Study the Moon's number 2 influence for 2010.

Outlines of the year number ruled by each planet are given below. Enjoy!

1 is the year of the Sun

Overview

The Sun is the brightest object in the heavens and rules number 1 and the sign of Leo. Because of this the coming year will bring you great success and popularity.

You'll be full of life and radiant vibrations and are more than ready to tackle your new nine-year cycle, which begins now. Any new projects you commence are likely to be successful.

Your health and vitality will be very strong and your stamina at its peak. Even if you happen to have the odd problem with your health, your recuperative power will be strong.

You have tremendous magnetism this year so social popularity won't be a problem for you. I see many new friends and lovers coming into your life. Expect loads of invitations to parties and fun-filled outings. Just don't take your health for granted as you're likely to burn the candle at both ends.

With success coming your way, don't let it go to your head. You must maintain humility, which will make you even more popular in the coming year.

Love and pleasure

This is an important cycle for renewing your love and connections with your family, particularly if you have children. The Sun is connected with the sign of Leo and therefore brings an increase in musical and theatrical activities. Entertainment and other creative hobbies will be high on your agenda and bring you a great sense of satisfaction.

Work

You won't have to make too much of an effort to be successful this year because the brightness of the Sun will draw opportunities to you. Changes in work are likely and, if you have been concerned that opportunities are few and far between, 2010 will be different. You can expect some sort of promotion or an increase in income because your employers will take special note of your skills and service orientation.

Improving your luck

Leo is the ruler of number 1 and, therefore, if you're born under this star sign, 2010 will be particularly lucky. For others, July and August, the months of Leo, will bring good fortune. The 1st, 8th, 15th and 22nd hours of Sundays especially will give you a unique sort of luck in any sort of competition or activities generally. Keep your eye out for those born under Leo as they may be able to contribute something to your life and may even have a karmic connection to you. This is a particularly important year for your destiny.

Your lucky numbers in this coming cycle are 1, 10, 19 and 28.

2 is the year of the Moon

Overview

There's nothing more soothing than the cool light of the full Moon on a clear night. The Moon is emotional and receptive and controls your destiny in 2010. If you're able to use the positive energies of the Moon, it will be a great year in which you can realign and improve your relationships, particularly with family members.

Making a commitment to becoming a better person and bringing your emotions under control will also dominate your thinking. Try not to let your emotions get the better of you throughout the coming year because you may be drawn into the changeable nature of these lunar vibrations as well. If you fail to keep control of your emotional life you'll later regret some of your actions. You must blend careful thinking with feeling to arrive at the best results. Your luck throughout 2010 will certainly be determined by the state of your mind.

Because the Moon and the sign of Cancer rule the number 2 there is a certain amount of change to be expected this year. Keep your feelings steady and don't let your heart rule your head.

Love and pleasure

Your primary concern in 2010 will be your home and family life. You'll be finally keen to take on those renovations, or work on your garden. You may even think of buying a new home. You can at last carry out some of those plans and make your dreams come true. If you find yourself a little more temperamental than usual, do some extra meditation and spend time alone until you sort this out. You mustn't withhold your feelings from your partner as this will only create frustration.

Work

During 2010 your focus will be primarily on feelings and family; however, this doesn't mean you can't make great strides in your work as well. The Moon rules the general public and what you might find is that special opportunities and connections with the world at large present themselves to you. You could be working with large numbers of people.

If you're looking for a better work opportunity, try to focus your attention on women who can give you a hand. Use your intuition as it will be finely tuned this year. Work and career success depends upon your instincts.

Improving your luck

The sign of Cancer is your ruler this year and because the Moon rules Mondays, both this day of the week and the month of July are extremely lucky for you. The 1st, 8th, 15th and 22nd hours on Mondays will be very powerful. Pay special attention to the new and full Moon days throughout 2010.

The numbers 2, 11 and 29 are lucky for you.

3 is the year of Jupiter

Overview

The year 2010 will be a number 3 year for you and, because of this, Jupiter and Sagittarius will dominate your affairs. This is extremely lucky and shows you'll be motivated to broaden your horizons, gain more money and become extremely popular in your social circles. It looks like 2010 will be a fun-filled year with much excitement.

Jupiter and Sagittarius are generous to a fault and so, likewise, your open-handedness will mark the year. You'll be friendly and helpful to all of those around you.

Pisces is also under the rulership of the number 3 and this brings out your spiritual and compassionate nature. You'll become a much better person, reducing your negative karma by increasing your self-awareness and spiritual feelings. You will want to share your luck with those you love.

Love and pleasure

Travel and seeking new adventures will be part and parcel of your romantic life this year. Travelling to distant lands and meeting unusual people will open your heart to fresh possibilities of romance.

You'll try novel and audacious things and will find yourself in a different circle of friends. Compromise will be important in making your existing relationships work. Talk about your feelings. If you are currently in a relationship you'll feel an upswing in your affection for your partner. This is a perfect opportunity to deepen your love for each other and take your relationship to a new level.

If you're not yet attached to someone, there's good news for you. Great opportunities lie in store and a spiritual or karmic connection may be experienced in 2010.

Work

Great fortune can be expected through your working life in the next twelve months. Your friends and work colleagues will want to help you achieve your goals. Even your employers will be amenable to your requests for extra money or a better position within the organisation.

If you want to start a new job or possibly begin an independent line of business, this is a great year to do it. Jupiter looks set to give you plenty of opportunities, success and a superior reputation.

Improving your luck

As long as you can keep a balanced view of things and not overdo anything, your luck will increase dramatically throughout 2010. The important thing is to remain grounded and not be too airy-fairy about your objectives. Be realistic about your talents and capabilities and don't brag about your skills or achievements. This will only invite envy from others.

Moderate your social life as well and don't drink or eat too much as this will slow your reflexes and weaken your chances for success.

You have plenty of spiritual insights this year so you should use them to their maximum. In the 1st, 8th, 15th and 24th hours of Thursdays you should use your intuition to enhance your luck, and the numbers 3, 12, 21 and 30 are also lucky for you. March and December are your lucky months but generally the whole year should go pretty smoothly for you.

4 is the year of Uranus

Overview

The electric and exciting planet of the zodiac, Uranus, and its sign of Aquarius, rule your affairs throughout 2010. Dramatic events will surprise and at the same time unnerve you in your professional and personal life. So be prepared!

You'll be able to achieve many things this year and your dreams are likely to come true, but you mustn't be distracted or scattered with your energies. You'll be breaking through your own self-limitations and this will present challenges from your family and friends. You'll want to be independent and develop your spiritual powers and nothing will stop you.

Try to maintain discipline and an orderly lifestyle so you can make the most of these special energies this year. If unexpected things do happen, it's not a bad idea to have an alternative plan so you don't lose momentum.

Love and pleasure

You want something radical, something different in your relationships this year. It's quite likely that your love life will be feeling a little less than exciting so you'll take some important steps to change that. If your partner is as progressive as you'll be this year, then your relationship is likely to improve and fulfil both of you.

In your social life you will meet some very unusual people, whom you'll feel are especially connected to you spiritually. You may want to ditch everything for the excitement and passion of a completely new relationship, but tread carefully as this may not work out exactly as you expect it to.

Work

Technology, computing and the Internet will play a larger role in your professional life this coming year.

You'll have to move ahead with the times and learn new skills if you want to achieve success.

A hectic schedule is likely, so make sure your diary is with you at all times. Try to be more efficient and don't waste time.

New friends and alliances at work will help you achieve even greater success in the coming period. Becoming a team player will be even more important in gaining satisfaction from your professional endeavours.

Improving your luck

Moving too quickly and impulsively will cause you problems on all fronts, so be a little more patient and think your decisions through more carefully. Social, romantic and professional opportunities will come to you but take a little time to investigate the ramifications of your actions.

The 1st, 8th, 15th and 20th hours of any Saturday are lucky, but love and luck are likely to cross your path when you least expect it. The numbers 4, 13, 22 and 31 are also lucky for you this year.

5 is the year of Mercury

Overview

The supreme planet of communication, Mercury, is your ruling planet throughout 2010. The number 5, which is connected to Mercury, will confer upon you success through your intellectual abilities.

Any form of writing or speaking will be improved and this will be, to a large extent, underpinning your success. Your imagination will be stimulated by this planet, with many incredible new and exciting ideas coming to mind.

Mercury and the number 5 are considered somewhat indecisive. Be firm in your attitude and don't let too many ideas or opportunities distract and confuse you. By all means get as much information as you can to help you make the right decisions.

I see you involved with money proposals, job applications, even contracts that need to be signed, so remain as clear-headed as possible.

Your business skills and clear and concise communication will be at the heart of your life in 2010.

Love and pleasure

Mercury, which rules the signs of Gemini and Virgo, will make your love life a little difficult due to its changeable nature. On the one hand you'll feel passionate and loving to your partner, yet on the other you will feel like giving it all up for the excitement of a new affair. Maintain the middle ground.

Also, try not to be too critical with your friends and family members. The influence of Virgo makes you prone to expecting much more from others than they're capable of giving. Control your sharp tongue and don't hurt people's feelings. Encouraging others is the better path, leading to greater emotional satisfaction.

Work

Speed will dominate your professional life in 2010. You'll be flitting from one subject to another and taking on far more than you can handle. You'll need to make some serious changes in your routine to handle the avalanche of work that will come your way. You'll also be travelling with your work, but not necessarily overseas.

If you're in a job you enjoy then this year will give you additional successes. If not, it may be time to move on.

Improving your luck

Communication is the key to attaining your desires in the coming twelve months. Keep focused on one idea rather than scattering your energies in all directions and your success will be speedier.

By looking after your health, sleeping well and exercising regularly, you'll build up your resilience and mental strength.

The 1st, 8th, 15th and 20th hours of Wednesday are lucky so it's best to schedule your meetings and other important social engagements during these times. The lucky numbers for Mercury are 5, 14, 23 and 32.

6 is the year of Venus

Overview

Because you're ruled by 6 this year, love is in the air! Venus, Taurus and Libra are well known for their affinity with romance, love, and even marriage. If ever you were going to meet a soulmate and feel comfortable in love, 2010 must surely be your year.

Taurus has a strong connection to money and practical affairs as well, so finances will also improve if you are diligent about work and security issues.

The important thing to keep in mind this year is that sharing love and making that important soul connection should be kept high on your agenda. This will be an enjoyable period in your life.

Love and pleasure

Romance is the key thing for you this year and your current relationships will become more fulfilling if you happen to be attached. For singles, a 6 year heralds an important meeting that eventually leads to marriage.

You'll also be interested in fashion, gifts, jewellery and all sorts of socialising. It's at one of these social engagements that you could meet the love of your life. Remain available!

Venus is one of the planets that has a tendency to overdo things, so be moderate in your eating and drinking. Try generally to maintain a modest lifestyle.

Work

You'll have a clearer insight into finances and your future security during a number 6 year. Whereas previously you may have had additional expenses and extra distractions, your mind will now be more settled and capable of longer-term planning along these lines.

With the extra cash you might see this year, decorating your home or office will give you a special sort of satisfaction.

Social affairs and professional activities will be strongly linked. Any sort of work-related functions may offer you romantic opportunities as well. On the other hand, be careful not to mix up your workplace relationships with romantic ideals. This could complicate some of your professional activities.

Improving your luck

You'll want more money and a life of leisure and ease in 2010. Keep working on your strengths and eliminate your negative personality traits to create greater luck and harmony in your life.

Moderate all your actions and don't focus exclusively on money and material objects. Feed your spiritual needs as well. By balancing your inner and outer sides you'll see that your romantic and professional lives will be enhanced more easily.

The 1st, 8th, 15th and 20th hours on Fridays will be very lucky for you and new opportunities will arise for you at those times. You can use the numbers 6, 15, 24 and 33 to increase luck in your general affairs.

7 is the year of Neptune

Overview

The last and most evolved sign of the zodiac is

Pisces, which is ruled by Neptune. The number 7 is deeply connected with this zodiac sign and governs you in 2010. Your ideals seem to be clearer and more spiritually orientated than ever before. Your desire to evolve and understand your inner self will be a double-edged sword. It depends on how organised you are as to how well you can use these spiritual and abstract concepts in your practical life.

Your past hurts and deep emotional issues will be dealt with and removed for good, if you are serious about becoming a better human being.

Spend a little more time caring for yourself rather than others, as it's likely some of your friends will drain you of energy with their own personal problems. Of course, you mustn't turn a blind eye to the needs of others, but don't ignore your own personal requirements in the process.

Love and pleasure

Meeting people with similar life views and spiritual aspirations will rekindle your faith in relationships. If you do choose to develop a new romance, make sure there is a clear understanding of the responsibilities of one to the other. Don't get swept off your feet by people who have ulterior motives.

Keep your relationships realistic and see that the most idealistic partnerships must eventually come down to Earth. Deal with the practicalities of life.

Work

This is a year of hard work, but one in which you'll

come to understand the deeper significance of your professional ideals. You may discover a whole new aspect to your career, which involves a more compassionate and self-sacrificing side to your personality.

You'll also find that your way of working will change and you'll be more focused and able to get into the spirit of whatever you do. Finding meaningful work is very likely and therefore this could be a year when money, security, creativity and spirituality overlap to bring you a great sense of personal satisfaction.

Tapping into your greater self through meditation and self-study will bring you great benefits throughout 2010.

Improving your luck

Using self-sacrifice along with discrimination will be an unusual method of improving your luck. The laws of karma state that what you give, you receive in greater measure. This is one of the principal themes for you in 2010.

The 1st, 8th, 15th and 20th hours of Tuesdays are your lucky times. The numbers 7, 16, 25 and 34 should be used to increase your lucky energies.

8 is the year of Saturn

Overview

The earthy and practical sign of Capricorn and its ruler Saturn are intimately linked to the number 8, which rules you in 2010. Your discipline and far-sightedness will help you achieve great things in the coming year. With cautious discernment, slowly but surely you will reach your goals.

It may be that due to the influence of the solitary Saturn, your best work and achievement will be behind closed doors away from the limelight. You mustn't fear this as you'll discover many new things about yourself. You'll learn just how strong you really are.

Love and pleasure

Work will overshadow your personal affairs in 2010, but you mustn't let this erode the personal relationships you have. Becoming a workaholic brings great material successes but will also cause you to become too insular and aloof. Your family members won't take too kindly to you working 100-hour weeks.

Responsibility is one of the key words for this number and you will therefore find yourself in a position of authority that leaves very little time for fun. Try to make the time to enjoy the company of friends and family and by all means schedule time off on the weekends as it will give you the peace of mind you're looking for.

Because of your responsible attitude it will be very hard for you not to assume a greater role in your workplace and this indicates longer working hours with the likelihood of a promotion with equally good remuneration.

Work

Money is high on your agenda in 2010. Number 8 is a good money number according to the Chinese and this year is at last likely to bring you the fruits of your hard labour. You are cautious and resourceful in all your dealings and will not waste your hard-earned savings. You will also be very conscious of using your time wisely.

You will be given more responsibilities and you're likely to take them on, if only to prove to yourself that you can handle whatever life dishes up.

Expect a promotion in which you'll play a leading role in your work. Your diligence and hard work will pay off, literally, in a bigger salary and more respect from others.

Improving your luck

Caution is one of the key characteristics of the number 8 and is linked to Capricorn. But being overly cautious could cause you to miss valuable opportunities. If an offer is put to you, try to think outside the square and balance it with your naturally cautious nature.

Be gentle and kind to yourself. By loving yourself, others will naturally love you, too. The 1st, 8th, 15th and 20th hours of Saturdays are exceptionally lucky for you, as are the numbers 1, 8, 17, 26 and 35.

9 is the year of Mars

Overview

You are now entering the final year of a nine-year cycle dominated by the planet Mars and the sign of Aries. You'll be completing many things and are determined to be successful after several years of intense work.

Some of your relationships may now have reached their use-by date and even personal affairs may need to be released. Don't let arguments and disagreements get in the road of friendly resolution in these areas of your life.

Mars is a challenging planet, and this year, although you will be very active and productive, you may find others trying to obstruct the achievement of your goals. As a result you may react strongly to them, thereby creating disharmony in your workplace. Don't be so impulsive or reckless, and generally slow things down. The slower, steadier approach has greater merit this year.

Love and pleasure

If you become too bossy and pushy with friends this year you will just end up pushing them out of your life. It's a year to end certain friendships but by the same token it could be the perfect time to remove conflicts and thereby bolster your love affairs in 2010.

If you're feeling a little irritable and angry with those you love, try getting rid of these negative feelings through some intense, rigorous sports and physical activity. This will definitely relieve tension and improve your personal life.

Work

Because you're healthy and able to work at a more intense pace you'll achieve an incredible amount in the coming year. Overwork could become a problem if you're not careful.

Because the number 9 and Mars are infused with leadership energy, you'll be asked to take the reins of the job and steer your company or group in a certain direction. This will bring with it added responsibility but also a greater sense of purpose for you.

Improving your luck

Because of the hot and restless energy of the number 9, it is important to create more mental peace in your life this year. Lower the temperature, so to speak, and decompress your relationships rather than becoming aggravated. Try to talk with your work partners and loved ones rather than telling them what to do. This will generally pick up your health and your relationships.

The 1st, 8th, 15th and 20th hours of Tuesdays are the luckiest for you this year and, if you're involved in any disputes or need to attend to health issues, these times are also very good to get the best results. Your lucky numbers are 9, 18, 27 and 36.

LEO

2010:
Your Daily Planner

Fortify yourself with contentment, for this is an
impregnable fortress.

—Epictetus

According to astrology, the success of any venture or activity is dependent upon the planetary positions at the time you commence that activity. Electional astrology helps you select the most appropriate times for many of your day-to-day endeavours. These dates are applicable to each and every zodiac sign and can be used freely by one and all, even if your star sign doesn't fall under the one mentioned in this book. Please note that the daily planner is a universal system applicable equally to all *twelve* star signs. Anyone and everyone can use this planner irrespective of their birth sign.

Ancient astrologers understood the planetary patterns and how they impacted on each of us. This allowed them to suggest the best possible times to start various important activities. For example, many farmers still use this approach today: they understand the phases of the Moon, and attest to the fact that planting seeds on certain lunar days produces a far better crop than does planting on other days.

In the following section, many facets of daily life are considered. Using the lunar cycle and the combined strength of other planets allows us to work out the best times to do them. This is your personal almanac, which can be used in conjunction with any star sign to help optimise the results.

First, select the activity you are interested in, and then quickly scan the year for the best months to start it. When you have selected the month, you can finetune your timing by finding the best specific dates. You can then be sure that the planetary energies will be in sync with you, offering you the best possible outcome.

Coupled with what you know about your monthly and weekly trends, the daily planner is an effective tool to help you capitalise on opportunities that come your way this year.

Good luck, and may the planets bless you with great success, fortune and happiness in 2010!

Getting started in 2010

How many times have you made a new year's resolution to begin a diet or be a better person in your relationships? And, how many times has it not worked out? Well, part of the reason may be that you started out at the wrong time, because how successful you are is strongly influenced by the position of the Moon and the planets when you begin a particular activity. You will be more successful with the following endeavours if you start them on the days indicated.

Relationships

We all feel more empowered on some days than on others. This is because the planets have some power over us—their movement and their relationships to each other determine the ebb and flow of our energies. And, our levels of self-confidence and sense of romantic magnetism play an important part in the way we behave in relationships.

Your daily planner tells you the ideal dates for meeting new friends, initiating a love affair, spending time with family and loved ones—it even tells you the most appropriate times for sexual encounters.

You'll be surprised at how much more impact you will make in your relationships when you tune yourself in to the planetary energies on these special dates.

Falling in love/restoring love

During these times you could expect favourable energies to meet your soulmate or, if you've had difficulty in a relationship, to approach the one you love to rekindle both your and their emotional responses:

January	18, 20, 23, 24
February	15, 16, 20, 24
March	29
April	16
May	14, 17, 18, 19, 20, 23
June	14, 15, 16, 20, 21
July	12
August	10, 13, 14
September	9, 21, 22
October	8, 18, 19, 20
November	14, 15, 16, 19, 20, 21
December	13, 17, 18

Special times with friends and family

Socialising, partying and having a good time with those whose company you enjoy is highly favourable under the following dates. They are excellent to spend time with family and loved ones in a domestic environment:

January	6, 26, 27
February	12, 13, 14, 15, 16, 20, 24
March	11, 21, 22, 29, 30, 31
April	8
May	15, 16, 17, 18, 19, 20, 23, 24
June	1, 2, 3, 11, 12, 14, 15, 16, 20, 21, 29, 30
July	8, 9, 12, 17, 18, 26, 27
August	5, 6, 9, 10, 13, 14, 22, 23, 24
September	1, 2, 5, 9, 10, 18, 19, 20, 30
October	3, 19, 20, 25, 26, 30, 31
November	3, 4, 14, 15, 16, 22, 26, 27
December	2, 9, 10, 11, 19, 20, 24, 25

Healing or resuming relationships

If you're trying to get back together with the one you love or need a heart-to-heart or deep-and-meaningful discussion with someone, you can try the following dates to do so:

January	12, 13, 14, 15, 21, 22, 23, 24, 25
February	6
March	6, 31
April	2, 7, 8, 12, 16, 19, 23, 24, 25, 26

May	10, 11, 12, 13, 14, 15, 16, 17, 18, 19, 20, 21,22, 23, 24, 25, 26, 27, 28, 30
June	3, 8, 9, 10, 11, 12, 13, 14, 15, 16, 17, 21, 22, 23, 25, 26, 27, 28, 29, 30
July	1, 2, 3, 4, 5, 10, 11, 12, 13, 15, 16, 17, 18, 19, 20, 21, 22, 23, 28, 29, 30
August	1, 2, 3, 4, 5, 6, 9, 10, 13, 14, 15, 16, 20, 23, 25, 26, 27
September	2, 5, 9, 10, 13, 17, 18, 19, 20
October	1, 2, 3, 6, 12, 13, 14, 15, 20, 22, 23, 24, 25, 26, 27, 28, 29, 30, 31
November	3, 4, 5, 6, 7, 8, 9, 21, 27, 28, 29, 30
December	2, 3, 4, 6, 12, 13, 14, 17, 18, 19, 20, 21, 23, 24, 25

Sexual encounters

Physical and sexual energies are well favoured on the following dates. The energies of the planets enhance your moments of intimacy during these times:

January	1, 6, 7, 21, 22
February	6, 12, 13, 14, 20, 24
March	14, 15, 17, 18, 19, 30, 31
April	23, 24, 25, 26
May	9, 12, 14, 17, 18, 19, 20
June	3, 8, 9, 10, 11, 14, 15, 16, 20, 21, 29, 30
July	8, 9, 10, 11, 12
August	6, 10, 13, 14, 22, 23, 24

September	3, 4, 5, 6, 9, 10, 18, 19, 20, 21, 22, 30
October	1, 2, 3, 7, 8, 18, 19, 20, 23, 24, 28, 29, 30, 31
November	3, 4, 14, 15, 16, 19, 24, 25, 26, 27
December	2, 10, 11, 12, 13, 15, 16, 17, 19, 20, 22, 23, 24, 25

Health and wellbeing

Your aura and life force are susceptible to the movements of the planets—in particular, they respond to the phases of the Moon.

The following dates are the most appropriate times to begin a diet, have cosmetic surgery, or seek medical advice. They also indicate the best times to help others.

Feeling of wellbeing

Your physical as well as your mental alertness should be strong on these following dates. You can plan your activities and expect a good response from others:

January	2, 3, 4, 5, 6, 7, 11, 12, 13, 14, 16, 17, 18, 21, 22, 23, 24, 30, 31
February	1, 2, 7, 8, 15, 16, 17, 18, 19, 20, 21, 22, 23, 24, 25, 26, 27, 28
March	16, 17, 18, 19, 20, 22, 23, 24, 25, 26, 27, 28, 29
April	7, 13, 14, 16, 28
May	2, 11, 14, 25, 26
June	8, 22, 23, 26, 27, 28, 29, 30

July	4, 5, 8, 9, 12, 13, 14, 15, 16, 19, 20, 23, 24, 25
August	5, 6, 9, 10, 11, 12, 13, 15, 16, 20, 21
September	9, 10, 11, 12, 13, 16, 17, 21, 22, 24, 25, 28, 29, 30
October	3, 4, 5, 6, 7, 8, 9, 10, 13, 14, 15, 22
November	4, 5, 6, 10, 11, 19, 20, 21
December	7, 8, 17, 18, 28, 29

Healing and medicine

These times are good for approaching others who have expertise when you need some deeper understanding. They are also favourable for any sort of healing or medication and making appointments with doctors or psychologists. Planning surgery around these dates should bring good results.

Often giving up our time and energy to assist others doesn't necessarily result in the expected outcome. However, by lending a helping hand to a friend on the following dates, the results should be favourable:

January	1, 2, 3, 4, 6, 7, 8, 9, 11, 12, 13, 14, 15, 16, 17, 18, 19, 20, 21, 22, 23, 24, 26, 27, 28, 29, 30, 31
February	1, 5, 6, 9, 11, 12, 13, 14, 15, 16, 19
March	1, 2, 3, 4, 5, 8, 9, 10, 11, 12, 18, 19, 24, 25, 29
April	1, 3, 4, 5, 22, 26
May	4, 5

June	1, 2, 3, 9, 10, 17, 18, 22, 23, 24, 25, 29, 30
July	6, 7, 15, 16, 17, 18, 19, 21, 22, 23, 24, 25, 26
August	2, 3, 4, 11, 12, 17, 18, 19, 20, 21, 30, 31
September	6, 7, 8, 10, 11, 12, 13, 14, 15, 16, 17, 18, 26, 27, 28, 29
October	5, 7, 8, 9, 10, 11, 12, 13, 14, 15, 16, 17, 18, 19, 20, 21, 22, 23, 24, 25, 26, 28, 29, 30, 31
November	1, 2, 3, 5, 7, 8, 10, 11, 14, 15, 17, 18, 19, 22, 23
December	4, 5, 7, 8, 9, 10, 12, 13, 14, 16, 23, 24, 25, 26, 28, 29, 30, 31

Money

Money is an important part of life, and involves many decisions—decisions about borrowing, investing, spending. The ideal times for transactions are very much influenced by the planets, and whether your investment or nest egg grows or doesn't grow can often be linked to timing. Making your decisions on the following dates could give you a whole new perspective on your financial future.

Managing wealth and money

To build your nest egg it's a good time to open your bank account or invest money on the following dates:

January	1, 6, 7, 13, 14, 15, 18, 21, 22, 28, 29
February	3, 4, 9, 10, 11, 12, 13, 14, 15, 17, 18, 24, 25

March	2, 3, 9, 10, 16, 17, 18, 23, 24, 29, 30, 31
April	5, 6, 7, 13, 14, 19, 20, 21, 26, 27,
May	2, 3, 4, 10, 11, 17, 18, 23, 24, 30, 31
June	6, 7, 8, 13, 14, 19, 20, 21, 26, 27, 28
July	4, 5, 10, 11, 12, 17, 18, 23, 24, 25, 31
August	1, 7, 8, 13, 14, 20, 21, 27, 28, 29
September	3, 4, 9, 10, 16, 17, 23, 24, 25
October	1, 2, 7, 8, 13, 14, 15, 21, 22, 28, 29
November	3, 4, 10, 11, 17, 18, 24, 25
December	1, 2, 7, 8, 14, 15, 16, 21, 22, 23, 24, 29

Spending

It's always fun to spend but the following dates are more in tune with this activity and are likely to give you better results:

January	3, 4, 5, 6, 7, 8, 9, 10, 11, 12, 13, 14
February	3, 4, 5, 10, 19
March	8, 10, 11, 13, 14, 19
April	7, 8, 11, 12, 22
May	6, 7, 8, 9, 10, 11, 12, 13, 17, 18, 19, 20, 21, 22, 23, 24, 25, 26, 27, 28
June	1, 11, 12, 14, 16, 17, 19, 23, 25, 26, 27, 28, 29, 30
July	6, 7, 8, 23, 24, 25, 26, 27, 28, 29, 31
August	1, 2, 3, 4, 5, 15, 16, 17, 18, 19, 30, 31
September	1, 2, 3, 4, 17, 18, 19, 20, 21, 22, 23, 27, 28, 29, 30

October	4, 7, 12, 13, 14, 15, 16, 17, 18, 19, 27, 28
November	2, 3, 4, 25, 26, 27, 28
December	11, 22, 23

Selling

If you're thinking of selling something, whether it is small or large, consider the following dates as ideal times to do so:

January	18
February	12, 13, 14, 15
March	5, 6, 9, 14, 15, 16, 17, 18, 19, 21
April	1, 3, 4, 5, 22, 26
May	7, 12, 21, 29
June	3, 8, 9, 10, 11, 12, 13, 17, 24, 25, 26, 27, 28, 30
July	1, 2, 7, 9, 10, 11, 25, 27, 28, 29, 30, 31
August	1, 2, 3, 4, 5, 6, 7, 8, 9, 10, 13, 20, 23, 28
September	2, 9, 10, 11, 12, 13, 14, 15, 16, 17, 18, 19, 20, 21, 22, 23, 24, 26, 30
October	1, 2, 3, 4, 6, 7, 10, 11, 17, 18, 19, 20, 21, 22, 23, 24, 25, 27, 29
November	3, 4, 5, 6, 7, 11, 14, 15, 16, 17, 18, 19, 21, 23, 24, 25, 26, 27, 28, 29, 30
December	1, 2, 3, 4, 5, 6, 7, 8, 9, 10, 11, 12, 13, 14, 15, 16, 17, 18, 19, 20, 21, 22

Borrowing

Few of us like to borrow money, but if you must, taking out a loan on the following dates will be positive:

January	12, 30
February	7, 12, 13
March	6, 7, 8, 11
April	3, 4, 8
May	9, 28, 29
June	1, 2, 3, 4, 5, 29, 30
July	1, 2, 3, 26, 27, 28, 29, 30
August	9, 25, 26
September	5, 6
October	3, 30
November	26, 27
December	3, 4, 21, 22, 23, 30, 31

Work and education

Your career is important, and continual improvement of your skills is therefore also crucial professionally, mentally and socially. The dates below will help you find out the most appropriate times to improve your professional talents and commence new work or education associated with your work.

You may need to decide when to start learning a new skill, when to ask for a promotion, and even when to make an important career change. Here are the days when your mental and educational power is strong.

Learning new skills

Educational pursuits are lucky and bring good results on the following dates:

January	15, 16, 17, 18, 19, 20, 21, 22, 25, 26, 27
February	14, 15, 16, 17, 18, 19, 22, 23, 28
March	16, 17, 18, 21, 22, 27, 28
April	17, 18, 24, 25
May	15, 16, 21, 22
June	12, 17, 18, 24, 25
July	15, 16, 21, 22, 23, 24, 25
August	11, 12, 17, 18, 19
September	8, 13, 15, 20, 21, 22
October	11, 12
November	7, 8, 9
December	6, 19, 20

Changing career path or profession

If you're feeling stuck and need to move into a new professional activity, changing jobs could be done at these times:

January	6, 7, 15, 16, 17, 23, 24
February	12, 13, 14, 19, 20, 21
March	19, 20, 27, 28
April	15, 16, 24, 25
May	14, 21, 22
June	17, 18, 19, 20, 21
July	8, 9, 15, 16, 23, 24, 25

August	5, 6, 11, 12, 20, 21, 22, 23
September	1, 2, 8, 13, 14, 15, 17
October	8, 13, 14, 15, 16, 17
November	3, 4, 10, 11, 19, 20, 21
December	1, 2, 3, 7, 8, 17, 18, 28, 29

Promotion, professional focus and hard work

To increase your mental focus and achieve good results from the work you do; promotions are also likely on these dates:

January	4, 5, 6, 11, 12, 13, 14, 15, 16, 17, 18, 19, 21
February	6
March	16, 17, 18, 19, 20, 21, 23, 24, 25, 26, 27, 28, 29
April	8, 28, 29
May	12, 21
June	25, 26, 27, 28
July	4, 5, 8, 9, 12, 13, 14, 15, 16, 17, 18, 19, 20, 21, 22, 23, 24, 25, 26, 27
August	5, 6, 10, 11, 12, 13, 14, 15, 16, 17, 18, 19, 20, 21, 22, 23, 24
September	13, 14, 15
October	10, 11, 12, 13, 14, 15, 17, 18, 19, 20, 22, 23, 24, 30, 31
November	2, 4, 5, 6, 7, 8, 9, 23, 24, 25, 26, 27, 28, 29, 30
December	2, 3, 4, 11, 12, 13, 14, 15, 16, 18, 19, 20, 21, 23, 24, 25

Travel

Setting out on a holiday or adventurous journey is exciting. Here are the most favourable times for doing this. Travel on the following dates is likely to give you a sense of fulfilment:

January	15
February	15, 16, 18, 19, 20, 21
March	16, 17, 18, 21, 22, 23
April	19, 24, 25, 26, 27
May	16, 17, 18, 21, 22
June	17, 18, 19, 20, 21, 24, 25
July	21, 22, 23, 24, 25
August	19
September	9, 21, 22
October	18, 19, 20, 21, 22
November	7, 16, 17, 18
December	6, 14, 16, 19, 20

Beauty and grooming

Believe it or not, cutting your hair or nails has a powerful effect on your body's electromagnetic energy. If you cut your hair or nails at the wrong time of the month, you can reduce your level of vitality significantly. Use these dates to ensure you optimise your energy levels by staying in tune with the stars.

Hair and nails

January	1, 2, 3, 4, 5, 6, 7, 8, 11, 12, 13, 14, 15, 18, 19, 20, 21, 22, 25, 26, 27
February	3, 4, 5, 7, 8, 15, 16, 17, 18, 19, 22, 23, 24, 25
March	2, 3, 4, 6, 7, 8, 14, 15, 21, 22
April	1, 2, 3, 4, 5, 10, 11, 12, 17, 18, 19, 20, 21, 22, 23, 28, 29, 30
May	1, 2, 3, 4, 5, 7, 8, 9, 10, 11, 12, 13, 15, 16, 17, 18, 25, 26 27, 28, 29, 30
June	4, 5, 11, 12, 14, 15, 16, 24, 25
July	1, 2, 3, 8, 9, 12, 13, 14, 21, 22, 28, 29, 30
August	1, 2, 5, 6, 17, 18, 19, 25, 26
September	1, 2, 6, 7, 14, 15, 21, 22, 23, 24, 28, 29, 30
October	3, 4, 11, 12, 18, 19, 20, 25, 26, 27, 28, 29, 30
November	7, 8, 9, 14, 15, 16, 22, 23, 24, 25, 26, 27
December	5, 6, 12, 13, 19, 20, 21, 22, 23, 24, 25

Therapies, massage and self-pampering

January	6, 7, 13, 14, 15, 18, 19, 20, 21
February	2, 3, 9, 11, 14
March	1, 9, 14, 16, 17, 20, 23, 29
April	4, 5, 6, 10, 11, 12, 13, 17, 25, 26
May	2, 3, 7, 8, 9, 10, 11, 14, 15, 16, 17, 22, 23, 24, 31
June	3, 5, 12, 18, 19, 26, 27
July	4, 7, 8, 9, 10, 16, 23, 28, 29, 30, 31
August	3, 4, 5, 6, 7, 13, 20, 21, 24, 25, 26, 27, 28, 31
September	2, 17, 21, 28, 29

October	13, 14, 15, 18, 19, 21, 25, 26, 27, 28
November	2, 3, 9, 11, 14, 15, 16, 17, 21, 24, 29
December	7, 12, 13, 14, 15, 18, 19, 20, 22, 26, 27, 28, 29

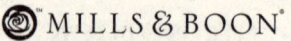